SURVIVING YOUR PARTNER'S JOB LOSS

SURVIVING YOUR PARTNER'S JOB LOSS

The Complete Guide to Rescuing Your Marriage and Family from Today's Economy

Jill Jukes and Ruthan Rosenberg
of
Murray Axmith & Associates Ltd.

National
Press
Books

Washington, D.C.

Library of Congress Cataloging-in-Publication Data

Jukes, Jill.
Surviving your partner's job loss: the complete guide to rescuing your marriage and family from today's economy
by Jill Jukes and Ruthan Rosenberg.
288 pp., 156 x 22.5 cm.
ISBN 1-882605-00-4
$12.95
Includes bibliographical references.
1. Unemployment—Psychological aspects.
2. Unemployed—Family relationships.
3. Work and family.
I. Rosenberg, Ruthan.
II. Title.
HD5708.J85   1993
331.13'7'019—dc20
92-46162
CIP

PRINTED IN THE UNITED STATES OF AMERICA

Acknowledgements

We are indebted to the many people who helped us bring this book to life. Our thanks to the Murray Axmith organization who sponsored, in full, the research and the writing of this book. We are proud to be a part of this progressive organization and are grateful to all our colleagues for their support and assistance during this project.

To our husbands, Hamilton and Murray, and our families, Shannon and Peter, and Alyse, Jill, Jordan and Michael, your love, encouragement and understanding made this book possible and carried us through the evenings and weekends we worked and missed being with you.

Above all, to the women and men who so generously allowed us into their lives and shared their experiences and knowledge with us, we say a heartfelt thank-you for giving us the opportunity to learn from you and to pass on your strength and wisdom.

Contents

Preface

We began our inquiry into the subject of this book with a basic assumption: that a marriage or other committed relationship is a partnership, not solely at home after work hours and on holidays and weekends, but 24 hours a day, 365 days a year. What happens to one member of that partnership involves the other. In the case of job loss, when one spouse is fired, the other is fired, too.

The process of getting rehired is also a partnership problem. Until now, however, assistance has only been available to that member of the partnership who actually lost the job, while the other is generally ignored. Yet, to succeed, each member of the partnership needs help to get through the trauma. With this in mind, we undertook to understand the experience of spouses who have been caught in such a situation and uncover those things that helped them to cope.

As with any such project, we had to limit the scope of our study. We chose to conduct our research within the context of the population to whom our outplacement consulting firm, Murray Axmith & Associates Ltd., provides the majority of its services. Therefore, we met with a large number of men and women whose partners' careers were at the professional, managerial and executive levels. We recognize that this group does not represent the total population and that people at different occupational levels may have concerns that we have not identified or addressed.

Similarly, although we would have liked to broaden the range of our work, time and feasibility constraints meant we could focus only on heterosexual relationships. Same-gender partners of people who have lost their jobs may have some additional perspectives of this experience, and we hope that any such information will soon come to light. Moreover, since completing our research and sharing our findings with numerous people, we have found that many of our results and suggestions also apply when one partner in a relationship is unemployed for reasons other than termination: for example, people who are looking for work after completing their education, have been retired from their companies, or are engaged in a job search after being disabled as a result of an accident or illness.

It is our belief that most people who, for whatever reason, are sharing the termination and job search experience with their mates will identify to some extent with the ideas contained in the following pages and, we hope, find them helpful.

To our knowledge, this is the first book about the partnership aspect of job loss and job search. We sincerely hope it will not be the last.

The Irony of the Two-Person Career

The Invisible Partner

Until very recently, it was not uncommon for young people to join a particular company and stay there until they retired. About the only way they could be dismissed from their jobs was to be caught with their fingers in the till or to commit an unforgivable blunder.

That no longer applies. Today in the United States and Canada, some three million executives, managers and professionals are fired from their jobs every year, and only a miniscule, almost negligible, number of them are let go for dishonesty or incompetence. The rest are victims of today's fiercely competitive, highly volatile business climate. You can scarcely pick up a newspaper without reading about the latest corporate mergers and how companies are being reorganized and downsized to make them leaner. And every time one company buys another or a firm decides to revitalize itself, the rules change. The new owners will invariably want to impose their own people and way of doing things on the new acquisition. In companies that are undergoing internal reorganization, similar changes take place, with new management teams and different corporate cultures emerging. In either case, the result is almost always the same: lots of people are suddenly declared irrelevant to the new scheme of things, and in many instances, otherwise valued and competent employees simply can't or won't fit in with the new style of doing business. That is how many of those three million executives, managers and professionals find themselves out on the street, usually with great sympathy from the media, their friends and even the people who fired them.

This book is about the spouses, who suffer through the disruptions of the dismissals and subsequent job searches as keenly as their mates—or even more so—but with little or no understanding from anyone.

Throughout this book, mainly for stylistic reasons, we will be using the words "wife," "husband," "spouse," "mate" and "partner" almost interchangeably. But this does not mean we've forgotten that many life partners are not officially married.

We fully realize that you yourself may also be an executive, a professional or a manager. And, although you may not have thought about it in this light, you are also your spouse's invisible partner. That is, in addition to furthering your own career, you undoubtedly contribute whatever is needed to help further your spouse's duties to his or her employer. In other words, your mate's job, and your own, is actually what we call a two-person career.

Think about it. How many times have you acted as a sounding board when your mate was having difficulty at work? How often has he or she sought your advice? How often have you given it?

If you are like the dozens of people we've interviewed, you have probably managed your own job, the household and the kids when the company needed your spouse. You may also have entertained his or her customers and colleagues, given of your time, your home and your hospitality as an enhancement to, or even an expected part of, your partner's job. Indeed, you may have actually moved your home to another city at the company's request. In all these and other ways, you have been an unofficial employee of the company—frequently unseen, probably unacknowledged and definitely unpaid. You may have even been part of the company's decision to hire your partner, perhaps even subjected to an interview before he or she was accepted for the job. Right or wrong, that act tacitly recognized your involvement in your partner's career; and, in all likelihood, it was the first and last such recognition.

Not only companies, but society as a whole, seems unaware of the contributions a life partner makes to an employee's career. In terms of a person's achievements, his or her spouse is virtually invisible. Moreover, this invisibility is so firmly rooted in our social fabric that, in most cases, the spouses themselves accept it unquestioningly and, as a result have tremendous difficulty articulating the deep sense of personal betrayal they feel when their partners are fired.

Insult Added to Injury Equals Isolation

When your partner is fired (even if the company let two hundred other people go the same day), it's a slap in the face, and the impact radiates outward, assaulting your sense of security, as well as your hopes, dreams and plans. All that was once known and predictable is now upset. From the moment that job disappears, your life is dramatically altered.

What happens to your routines when your mate is suddenly at home all day? How do you provide help and support when your own fears and worries seem so overwhelming? What will the dismissal mean for your own activities, career or educational plans?

There is no way around it: when they fired your partner, they slapped your face, too. That is the injury. The insult is that nobody seems to notice. Most likely no one has even thought about offering any assistance to help you cope with the effects of the termination. Most of the attention and sympathy extended by others is directed toward your mate, and there is no doubt that this support is needed. Yet few people, perhaps not even you, recognize that this crisis is your crisis too. For all intents and purposes, you have been fired too, but your hurt and confusion are somehow imperceptible. The result is a feeling of utter isolation.

It's a societal error of omission. People don't mean to exclude your from their concern. It simply does not occur to them that there is any reason to be worried about you. Of course, this oversight is aggravated by an expectation that you will be consistently loving, caring, understanding and supportive of your mate. Probably, it is an expectation that you have of yourself. In fact, this attitude is so pervasive in our society, you may not realize that while others are inquiring about your partner's well-being, no one is asking how you are doing!

Feeling isolated is not necessarily a short-term thing. What happens to you when your spouse's job search stretches beyond a month or two? Or six or eight months, or even far beyond that? What do you do when fear and worry overcome your optimism? How do you handle the negative feelings that, try as you might, you cannot suppress? And what do you do with the guilt that almost invariably accompanies these emotions?

For most people, this is uncharted territory. But the truth is, many hundreds of thousands of others have traveled this ground before you. Although at times terribly painful, your reaction to your partner's firing is a phenomenon that is describable, explainable and perfectly normal. It affects your attitudes and plays havoc with your feelings. Yet it is also one of those rough passages through life that can be successfully navigated.

We have taken this trip with dozens of people, and we have written our book with two primary purposes in mind. First, we want you to know that virtually any emotion you are likely to feel has already been experienced by countless others in similar circumstances. Second, we want you to be assured that this is not uncharted territory, and although it may often seem so, the trip across it is not endless. Thus our book is ultimately a guide to how you can cope with the rigors of the journey and, as almost all people do, arrive at the end of it a hardier, stronger person with a keener insight into your own emotions and a much better understanding of your mate and your relationship.

Finally, before we begin, we must add that we, the authors, are not in fact your guides. That honor belongs to the dozens of generous men and women who gave many hours of their time helping us to understand what they have been through.

In the following pages, they largely tell their own stories in their own words, with our role being primarily that of editors of their accounts and synthesizers of the countless lessons they taught us. We have much to thank them for, and trust that you will too.

Chapter One

What's Happening to Me?

To ensure our subjects' privacy, they have all been given different names, and certain biographical details have been altered.

We first met Leslie when she and her husband, Paul, came in to talk to our financial counselor about their immediate and long-term future. Only two days before, Paul had been dismissed from his position as a high-level manager at one of the oil companies. As part of his severance package, the firm had hired the outplacement consulting firm that we work for to help him search for a new job. One of the services we provide is financial counseling, which our company believes should begin immediately after termination.

Although he tried to put up a brave front with corny jokes and an offhand manner, Paul, quite understandably, was still clearly shellshocked by his sudden dismissal. Hardly forty-eight hours earlier, at 3:30 in the afternoon, with no previous warning, he had been summoned to the office of the vice president and bluntly told that he was out. Apart from a few words about how he was no longer a good fit, he was offered no explanation of the sudden action. A security guard watched as he gathered up a few personal possessions and then, in full view of all Paul's colleagues, some of whom he had worked with for twenty years, the guard escorted him out of the building.

Except for the escort out to the street, Paul's firing is fairly typical. No one escapes being devastated by the experience, though few are as visibly shattered as Paul was.

In distinct contrast, Leslie was everything a wounded husband would want a nurturing, supportive spouse to be. Wearing a superbly cut navy-blue suit, she looked exactly like the person she normally was: an extremely competent mother, a very good credit manager and an exemplary company wife. Though she bristled a bit when the financial counselor suggested that their daughters' credit cards be put on hold for the time being and that she and Paul take their vacation a bit closer to home than planned, it was obvious that she was not there for herself. She was there to prop up Paul, and she was doing it very well. Anyone looking at her would have thought his dehiring had not wounded her at all, and that she was treating the situation as just another passing household crisis.

But when we got to know her better, we soon learned that there was a lot more happening to Leslie than met the eye. For although we call ourselves outplacement consultants and we use euphemisms like "dismissal," "decruiting," "termination," "dehiring" and so forth, what all these words mean is "fired." Moreover, as we have discovered time and time again, when people are fired, more often than not, their partners are equally devastated, and, as the invisible partners in their mates' careers, they suffer a welter of deep and conflicting emotions that they and everyone else concerned tend to think are irrelevant to the immediate situation.

But they are not.

"I was mad at him," Leslie told us later. "You want to blame somebody, and in the back of your mind you're thinking, What the heck did he do? Why did he let this happen? So there is anger toward your husband, then guilt that you are mad at him. So there is this cover-up— you have to keep it inside, because this is not the time to get mad. He's so devastated and so fragile that if you come out and attack him you won't solve anything."

Murray, a stockbroker and one of the first male spouses we interviewed, said almost the same thing. His wife was let go after her employer's firm was bought by another. "Adele had told me about the merger or whatever it was, and I'd got the impression she wasn't too keen on the new president, but I thought everything was fine," Murray said. "Then one day there's Adele waiting for me at the place where I always have lunch, which is twenty miles from where she worked, so right away I knew something was wrong, and I was right. The new guy had booted her out, and I didn't know what to think. I mean, I had too much to think about. For one thing, she's in artificial intelligence, and there's not too many places that do that kind of work, so I knew right off the bat Adele might have to look for work out of town, and what if she found a job in Boston or someplace? Which got me wondering what she'd done to turn the new guy off, which made me angry at her. But I couldn't say anything, of course, because I could see Adele was a wreck and needed my sympathy. So there I was, trying to comfort her and feeling like a creep for being mad at her."

This is the crux of the spouse's dilemma. The terminated partner desperately needs care and support, and the spouse feels impelled to provide it. But at the same time the spouse, too, needs help and support, particularly in contending not only with the anger he or she is bottling up, but also the welter of other emotions that spouses often believe they should not feel and dare not talk about, either with their partners or anyone else.

We, however, are going to discuss these dire and important needs. To get us started, we have compiled a list of the more common emotions that beset people when the unthinkable happens and their mates are suddenly without a job. We have also included comments by people who have experienced these emotions and occasional tips on how to deal with the various feelings that may arise. At the end of this section, as at the end of every chapter but two, there are further suggestions to help you with the everyday process of coping.

The primary emotions are:

Shock and Disbelief

Virtually every person we talked to experienced these two emotions, even when they had some advance warning and were expecting the axe to fall. Most, however, were not expecting it. One of the most poignant examples was Carol Ann, the wife of a vice president of a pipe company. Twenty years earlier, she and Colin had been part of a group of two dozen young managers and their wives sent to America by their Belgian parent company to open a branch plant. The plant prospered and had recently been sold to another company.

"They took over on March 12," Carol Ann says. "I had lunch with a friend the next week. Her husband was an executive at the firm, too. I mentioned that Colin was having his interview with the new president that day. She said, 'I know. Bert's is tomorrow,' and I sort of took a bite and said, 'Wouldn't it be awful if he was fired?' and we giggled because it was such a preposterous idea. That evening, Colin came home and I rushed to the door and said, 'How did it go?' He said, 'Oh, fine, fine,' and he walked in and said, 'We're free.' I said, 'What do you mean, we're free?' and he said, 'They don't want me to work with them anymore.' Until then, he'd been putting on a brave show for me, but as soon as he said that, his face just fell apart. It was the most dreadful shock of my life. I get quite cold thinking about it even now. I never thought that would happen after so many years with the firm."

The unfortunate truth is that, these days, it can happen to anybody at any time. Cheryl, the wife of a vice president of a big international packaged goods company, learned about her husband's release in an airport parking lot. She and their children were returning from a vacation in Mexico. He had come to pick them up, but there was no room in the trunk of his car for their bags.

"It was full of the files and pictures he had at work," Cheryl says. Our eldest boy said, 'What's that?' and Glen said, 'That's my office. That's it.' I knew he had talked about leaving, but until then it just hadn't registered—until we saw his office in the trunk of the car. I don't know whether I took it too well."

Cheryl's case is a good illustration of how ambiguous these situations can get. She had been aware that her husband was not getting along with the new president and wanted to leave. But it had never occurred to her that he would ask for his release from a secure, extremely well-paid job. But that's what happened. The new president had offered her husband a number of unsatisfactory positions within the company and he rejected them all. It was clear to him that they didn't really want him around any more. Finally, while Cheryl and the kids were away, he decided he'd had enough and, much to his wife's subsequent surprise, negotiated a settlement and walked out the door.

Cheryl, like many spouses we've met, completely ignored some very clear warning signs that her partner's release was imminent. And, although it might not seem so at first, Murray belongs in this category, too. From his experience in the business world he knew that heads often roll after one company acquires another, but it never occurred to him that this might apply to his wife, even though he received a very distinct signal in Adele's opinion of the new president.

The reality of Glen's situation did not hit Cheryl until she saw the office supplies in the back of his car, and she was devastated. The fact that his exit had been voluntary was beside the point, and the aftereffects of the shock, especially her bitterness toward the man who had driven her husband out of the company, still lingered when we talked to her four years later.

Relief

Even spouses who are well prepared for their mates' release can still find the actual event a shock, or at least a matter of grave concern; but this is frequently followed by a profound feeling of relief, which can last a few hours or a few weeks, though usually only until the realities of the job search come into play. Relief is particularly likely if the spouse dislikes the mate's job or boss, if the job has been a source of dissatisfaction—or if the firing has come after weeks or even months of waiting for the inevitable.

Mary Ellen, a homemaker and volunteer worker, told us how her husband, Derek, was fired after a tiring year of internal political turmoil and uncertainty at the auto manufacturer where he was the vice president of sales. She was ready. "I knew how I was going to behave, but how would he react? When the day came, he took it very well and that night they went out to dinner with his brother. We had a few drinks and it was all quite cheery. But that short period of euphoria didn't go on too long. The next morning, we were back to reality, and Derek was out looking for a job."

A somewhat similar tale is told by Jennifer, a free-lance graphics artist, whose husband was released from a position as vice president of marketing for a large consumer products company: "Rumors had been flying for about six months before they actually got to the termination. So that for us was the really hard part, because one day Stewart was going to be out and then another day he'd be in. A lot of people resigned, but we decided that he'd been there sixteen years, and if they wanted him to leave, they'd damn well have to tell him. Anyway, it was not a pleasant time in that office, and when he finally got the word, my first reaction really was relief because we finally knew where he stood, and he was basically quite happy with his compensation package. One of the first things he said to me was 'I do have a job, and that's looking for a job.'

"Within two weeks, we'd bought a computer and a desk and set up an office in the storage room at home. I was just a wreck from his demands. Everything that'd been in the storage room was piled in the hall. My answering machine wasn't good enough, and we had to get one with a telephone that didn't take up so much room on the desk. I mean, he was so geared up by the time he was terminated that he had all this energy just pouring out to do things and get his resumé going and get talking to people and seriously considering his next job."

To Jennifer's further relief, Stewart found a new job within two weeks, which is an exceptionally short search period. But the point to be made here is that although terminations are welcomed with relief by some spouses, a more frequent reaction, after the initial shock has passed, is either or both of two distinct forms of anger.

Anger at the Company

It can be risky, but this is the easiest anger for spouses to handle.

They can become enraged at the company for hurting their partners, for the disruption of their lives that dismissal causes and for not providing them or their mates with assistance to cope with the crisis. Often they are enraged for all of these reasons. Listen to only four of the many spouses who might have been quoted here.

Carl, a salesman with a growing lubricants recycling firm, was only beginning to get his new career off the ground when his wife, Shannon, was fired after fifteen years of service with a record company. Although the couple had dated on and off for many years, they had been married only ten months, and Shannon was three months pregnant. "Five years ago, I lost the small clothing store I owned," Carl told us. "After that, I tried all sorts of things, until I found this job. Things started looking up for me and we decided to settle down and start a family. We began saving for a house, and with Shannon's salary and my commissions getting bigger and bigger every month, I figured we'd be able to make it happen in a couple of years. But six months ago, her company started to reorganize. She warned me that she might be let go. In fact, she was putting her files in order and so forth, just in case that happened. When it did, I was on the road, so I found out when I called home. I tried not to let it show, but I was bloody angry. How could they do that to someone who'd been with them so long, somebody who'd worked so hard and put in so many extra hours and had made a real contribution to the company? On top of it all, she was pregnant, and I was worried about how her being fired would affect the baby."

Bob, a software designer on contract with a steel company, whose wife, Estelle, was vice president of operations for a large chain of children's wear shops has a similar story: "Estelle had always been in on previous downsizing decisions, but not this one. The president scheduled a meeting with her and another colleague, but when she arrived, the guy wasn't there. She asked, 'Where's Dan?' and the president said, 'I'm sorry, I lied to you. Dan's not coming. We're doing some more downsizing and here's your package.' He talked to her for about five minutes, then shuffled her off to collect her things. She was really upset and didn't learn till later that day that the rest of her team was let go, too. I'm still ticked off at the way they handled it. After all those years, why couldn't they have at least let her stay and finish the projects she had going?"

Cheryl, who had learned about her husband's release at the airport, was furious with the company president: "That pompous nerd. How dare he do this after making such idiotic demands on my husband for the past year. He said the way to turn the company around was for Glen and everyone else to work twenty-two hours a day and sleep for two. He actually said, 'I don't want your wife and children to know what you look like!' And now to do this."

And then there's Maggie, a homemaker, whose husband was a senior manager at a large, profitable telecommunications company. She went with him to a prestigious company affair in Hawaii. When they returned, he was given a performance bonus of fifty thousand dollars, and two weeks later they fired him. "So it was a shock," Maggie says. "It devastated me for Doug, and I think he thought I was going to turn around and say to him, 'What did you do wrong? Why did you do it?' I didn't. I was angry, mind you. When the shock wore off, I was very angry, but toward the company, not Doug, because I feel that I know him. We've been married nineteen years, and he gives his all. I mean he was there all night if he had to be. Maybe he was a workaholic. I think he regrets that now. Although he's still young, he's missed a lot of our life because he was at work all the time."

Anger at Your Mate

As with Leslie and Murray, most people find it extremely uncomfortable to be angry at their mates, but the feeling arises from three basic issues. The first is because the partner has lost the job. This anger, however, rarely emerges as outright rage.

For example, Angie, a part-time designer, whose husband had been the director of systems development for a utility company, didn't even realize she was angry until she was talking to a friend whose husband had gone through the same thing a year earlier.

"Apparently their marriage almost came apart," Angie says, "and she mentioned something I hadn't consciously thought about, but I think it really was bothering me, and that is the anger you feel toward your husband. I was trying to think I shouldn't feel that way, but you do. You feel an anger toward him, and apparently it was really strong with Tina. I find it is strong, too. And since she brought it up that day, I've been thinking, 'Oh, gosh, that's what's been bugging me,' but it's not something you can talk to your husband about particularly. But it really comes through at times, and you get so angry and you think, 'How did he let this happen? Where was he? Why wasn't he more aware of what was going on?' "

Similar anger toward and suspicions about her husband's political savvy were also voiced by Karen, a sociologist, whose husband was suddenly bounced from his job as a cost accountant with a tire manufacturer. "I'm not really blaming Gil for what happened," she told us. "At the same time, I don't think things like that just happen. I really don't. I don't know whether he could have prevented it, but he sure could have left before it happened." In short, she's mad at Gil for not reading the writing on the wall. And she may be justifiably angry. In the course of our research, we found many instances where terminated employees had not seen, or ignored, signs that a shakeup was imminent. By the same token, we also met several spouses, like Murray and Cheryl, who ignored some extremely loud hints of impending trouble in their partners' jobs. This is a very complex matter, and we deal with it later, in the coping notes and the next chapter.

The second type of anger that must be addressed is the hostility spouses feel when their partners are (or seem to be) not working fast enough to find a new job. In many cases they will be correct in concluding that their partners have become lethargic in their job searches or overly rigid in the types of jobs they are willing to consider. Or they, like far too many spouses, may simply not understand what a job search entails. Accordingly, we have devoted two complete chapters to the focal points of these issues. Chapter three, What's Happening to My Partner?, deals with the emotions people experience when they are fired. And chapter four, The Job Search, describes the mechanics of a thorough hunt for work, which can, through no fault of your mate's, take up to a year or more.

The third major cause of anger is the way a firing can disrupt and threaten a couple's customary roles in their relationship. Again the issue is just too complex to deal with in this short list. In fact, the rest of this book concerns understanding and coping with the manifold effects of a firing on your relationship. To that end, we will be dealing not only with anger, but with the many other emotions, issues and circumstances that arise, including several surprisingly positive opportunities that the experience may offer.

Bewilderment

A lot of anger is rooted in plain confusion. Over and over again, people told us that they simply did not know why their partners had been fired. In many cases, the companies did not provide specific reasons. In other cases, their partners weren't especially communicative.

Whatever the case, the *why?* continues to haunt the spouse long after the firing, and sometimes another, rather insidious, factor can creep into the equation. That is, no one is more aware of a mate's shortcomings than his or her spouse, and when a job loss occurs, a spouse may begin to wonder if these shortcomings were the cause of the dismissal and all the subsequent disruptions.

"You're always thinking about it," says Stephanie, who was a homemaker when her husband was fired from his job as audit manager of a large accounting firm. "You are always dealing with it. Like, sometimes I question myself and think, was he really let go because of budget cuts or was he not the right person there? I would never say that to him, but you do wonder."

Shame and Embarrassment

Clare, a teacher, told us about how she and her husband reacted when he became one of the very early victims of downsizing in the tobacco industry: "We didn't want to tell anybody, because we were one of the first couples it happened to, and it's not supposed to happen if you work hard and go to work day after day and do your job well and get good performance reviews. You figure you're just going to stay with the company forever. I mean, my dad retired from the hospital and Les's father is retired from Bell after being there a zillion years. Those were the only jobs they ever had."

Clare's story is a good example of how pervasive the old way of regarding a job as a lifetime thing still is. It is also a good illustration of how firmly the stigma of being fired is rooted in our culture, despite dramatically changing economic conditions. Almost every person we spoke with mentioned that one of their first concerns was who they were going to tell about the firing, and some even wondered whether they should tell anyone at all! In some cases, it was a question of how, or whether, to tell their parents. This is quite understandable, because in our parents' day being fired was indeed taken as a moral blot on a person's character. But we also encountered many couples who were reluctant to tell their family and friends, and they often delayed breaking the news for absurdly long periods of time.

There are very few areas where we can offer blanket advice, but this is one of them, and our advice is, *do it now*. You may want to take a couple of days to catch your breath, of course, but if you tell family and friends about the firing reasonably soon, you won't have all the trouble of maintaining the story that your spouse still has a job, which will be one less worry on your plate. Also, the more people who know that your spouse is looking for a job, the better the odds of finding one will be, for friends and relatives can often be very good contacts for new job opportunities. Finally, it is just plain silly to try to hide the dismissal, because it is bound to backfire. Almost inevitably, someone is going to call the former workplace and be told, "Oh, Marcia hasn't worked here for months." Your secret will be all over town before the day is out.

There are also, we should add, situations where people have such high-profile jobs that their firing is widely reported in the media. Their mates might be plagued by embarrassment here, as well. The event is so public that they have no control over who knows, and this increases their feeling of helplessness, exposure and shame.

Guilt by Association

As we have noted, despite the new economic realities, many people still feel that their mates' dismissals reflect badly on them. In some cases, spouses are so intellectually and emotionally involved in their partners' careers that they experience a dismissal as an equal failure on their part.

Then there are extreme cases in which someone is let go for dishonesty or gross incompetence. The spouses in these situations will often feel guilty, too, as if, by virtue of their relationship, they are partners in crime. They suddenly see their mates in a startling new light and wonder if they can ever trust their own judgment again.

In one situation that came to our attention, an executive was embezzling money from his employer. The end result was criminal charges being filed against him and a considerable bit of negative publicity. The man's wife was not only devastated and shamed by his arrest, but also left wondering why she had never seen any signs of his potential for this type of behavior, and if she could ever trust him again. She shared his public disgrace, as well, and on top of it all was terribly worried about how the scandal would affect their children.

Profound Disappointment

This can take many forms, but is primarily expressed as disappointment over the many things that suddenly have to be canceled or at least put on hold, including vacations, renovations to the house and so forth. Cheryl deeply regretted her loss of the status, perks and vibrant social life that went with being the wife of a vice president of a big-name company. But above all, she regretted the seemingly wasted years: "When he first mentioned leaving the company, I said, 'I'll be happy with whatever you decide.' But then, when he was released, I thought, 'he'd made it to the top, and from there he could've become president of the company or rotated within the parent organization, which is into all sorts of interesting things, like television. So he spent all these years climbing to that level, and for what?' That's how I looked at it. 'For what?'

Carl, who was finally getting some stability in his life, saw his hopes for the future begin to fade with Shannon's firing from the record company. "With the baby coming, she won't be able to even start looking for work for at least nine or ten months. She's been dreaming about buying a house as much as I have, but now who knows when, or even if, that will ever happen?"

Anxiety and Fear

Few areas of a person's life are free from anxieties once his or her mate has been fired. Fears abound, about everything from possible changes in lifestyle to worries about economic security, marital relationships, children's education and general well-being, and his or her own plans and social relationships. Again the topic is simply too big to be dealt with adequately within the limits of this list. So suffice it to say that in one way or another, almost all the situations, stories and coping notes in the following pages relate, to varying degrees, to one or more of the nearly infinite kinds of anxiety-causing issues.

Vulnerability

This emotion goes hand in hand with anxiety about possible changes. Their mates' job loss brings home to people just how much they depend on their spouses' income and just how vulnerable they are when it is discontinued. For some, the firing completely shatters their sense of security. In most cases (especially after the mate has found a new job), the intensity of this feeling wanes, but some people never feel completely secure again.

It's still too early to tell about Pat, a homemaker, whose husband was, until one late winter afternoon, the director of human resources for a specialty chemical company. "He called about twenty minutes before I had to take our youngest to the doctor," Pat told us. "I was very sad, very angry and feeling powerless, I guess. The family's lot is very attached to his job and, when he loses it, you can feel quite put down and vulnerable. When I got to the doctor's, the nurse thought I had pink eye. I was really flustered and devastated, you know, just sort of holding the fort till Mark got home. And I was on the verge of blurting out what had happened to the nurse."

Later, we'll talk about the benefits of being able to share your worry with others. The issue here is vulnerability. Even people who are well entrenched in their own careers feel extremely vulnerable when their mates are fired, but there is something special about the link between a full-time homemaker like Pat and her husband's job. It is, besides her source of livelihood, a portion of her identity.

Ian provides a good example of how a well-entrenched career person can suddenly feel vulnerable when his or her mate is terminated. He and Victoria are a fast-tracking, ambitious couple. When she was fired, they had just made the down payment on a house that was being custom-built for them. "The builder said it would be ready in September," Ian told us. "Victoria was let go in May, and she was still out of work in July. She'd already refused one job offer, and I was starting to get really edgy. The completion of the house was getting closer every day, and in spite of Victoria's severance pay, we were going to need her salary to make our mortgage payments. I was afraid we were going to lose the house and, with it, our life savings."

Fortunately for Ian and Victoria, the completion of their home was delayed by several months, but that did not stop Ian from exerting an enormous amount of pressure on Victoria to find a job.

A Sense of Loss

Although it is their mates who have lost their jobs, spouses will often feel equally bereft. This is occasioned by the loss of predictable routines: loss of their mates' colleagues who were also friends, lifestyle losses, lost dreams, loss of the identity acquired through association with their mates' work, position and company, and loss of roots if a move to another community is necessary. Above all, that shattered sense of security represents, for some, a loss of innocence.

Angela, a teacher, mourned the loss of the company car her husband, Percy, used as a hotel chain's director of food and beverages. "It seemed," she said, "to be a symbol of everything else that was to follow. The first night was spent in tears. We both felt frozen, but the next day life continued. I was getting ready to go to work. Percy had to go back to his office to finalize the paperwork, and suddenly it dawned on us no car after today! That was unthinkable. We were stuck way out in the suburbs."

Depression

Depression flows from the losses noted earlier. Molly, a homemaker, told us that after her husband lost his job as the general manager of a security systems firm, she cried on and off for four days. "I was making him feel terrible, because there was nothing he could say or do to make me feel any better. He finally said, 'Molly, stop it! You're not doing yourself any good. This is what happened and we've got to accept it.' And I think he, more than anyone, snapped me out of it. I mean, at least I got it under control. These depressions come and go. You can't help it."

Excitement at New Opportunities

It's not all glum. A dismissal can also be an opportunity to reassess your lives together and consider new directions. Most couples realize this very quickly, with the result that every job interview your spouse goes to and every letter he or she writes can seem like the first step to a more satisfying life.

Disappointment at Rejections and Lost Opportunities

Unfortunately, unless he or she is unbelievably lucky, your mate will hear and receive many "no"s before getting that all-important "yes." No one can predict how long a job search will take, and the best way to cope with the highs and lows you'll experience along the way is to be prepared for them. Take a tip from the wiser major league baseball players. They are prepared for the fact that in the course of a 162-game season, besides some wonderful hitting streaks, they are also bound to have several slumps, and their most frequent advice, to their teammates and themselves, is "Never let yourself get too high. Never let yourself get too low."

Helplessness

Although your life is dramatically altered by your partner's dismissal, you cannot solve the basic problem. Only your mate can do that—by getting another job. At best, you will find this situation uncomfortable. At worst, it can lead to acute dismay at your own sense of helplessness.

Listen to Angie, whose frustration flowed from her belief that her husband was being woefully unrealistic in the types of jobs he was applying for: "I can go for two or three days and forget about it, and then all of a sudden you go through another two or three days where it's just on your mind constantly and you wake up at four in the morning and you start to think about it and you're still awake at six-thirty, when the alarm goes off. In fact, I think about it every morning when I wake up. It's the first thing I think about. You may forget in the night but then you think, oh, no, not another day of this."

Stress

This will vary according to the individual and depend on a number of factors: your financial situation, your own family's history of coping with stress, your health and that of the people close to you, the strength of your relationship with your partner, the amount of information about the job search that he or she shares, the length of the search, and any number of other external factors, including luck. Some of the people we talked to did not find the situation too stressful at all, while for others it was terrible, and some turned to prescription drugs and alcohol to help them cope.

Feelings Toward Your Own Work

Work is a blessing for many people in this situation. It provides the family with a paycheck and distraction from their worries. On the other hand, there are people who, when they suddenly become their families' sole breadwinners, feel trapped in jobs they had hitherto enjoyed. All of a sudden it isn't a matter of "I love to work." It's now, "I have to work."

We also met people who had become extremely self-conscious about having a job when their partners did not. Ian was one of them. "I'm in a high-pressure job," he said. "I spend a lot of hours at it, travel a fair amount, and my career is not only important to me, it's my way of having fun. When Victoria was looking for work, it was a difficult time for her, and I felt guilty about how well things were going for me and how much I was enjoying myself while she was so unhappy."

Some people who felt the way Ian did stopped talking about their work, they no longer brought work home, and, whenever possible, avoided traveling for their companies. A few even told us they dreaded getting a promotion before their partners had found new jobs, fearing that success would further demoralize their mates. Some people were also haunted by the enormous decisions they would have to make if their spouses sought or accepted work in another city or country.

One woman told us that she had always been a risk taker in her career, until her husband lost his job. Overnight she became very cautious, fearing that the same thing could happen to her and eliminate their only source of income.

Fantasies of Magical Solutions

A common such fantasy is meeting the right person at a cocktail party, who hires your spouse on the spot. Again, these dreams are fun and a necessary release mechanism, but we must add that we found only one job seeker who won this way. Theresa's husband, Ray, met the president of a company at a gathering at a cottage and was hired in a dream position four days later. We also have to add that this meeting took place only after Ray's job search had gone on fourteen months. And the real reason he got the job was that he and his wife had not been shy about telling people he had been fired. The hostess, knowing this and being a good hostess, simply introduced him to the president because this man had gone through a firing a few years earlier, and she thought he and Ray would have something in common to talk about.

Fantasies of Revenge

These thoughts range from telling off your mate's former boss the next time you see him to having a load of manure dumped into his brand-new Mercedes convertible. Our best advice here is *don't do it*. Fantasies can of course be fun, and you and your spouse might get a well-needed giggle out of your more outrageous ones. But actually doing or saying anything will almost always backfire, creating negative impressions of both of you, which won't help the job search at all. This is one of the cases where keeping your most secret thoughts to yourself is the wisest course.

Betrayal

Similar to loss, betrayal is more searing. It's as if the company has broken an unwritten contract with you, the invisible partner, who invested a huge amount of your time, hopes and future in your mate's job. To take one rather vivid example, Carol Ann, from Belgium, whom we mentioned earlier, came to America only because of her husband's job at the pipe plant. The other executives and their wives were an extended family, and her and Colin's retirement plans were based on another ten years' service with the company. When he was fired, she matched his brave show with one of her own. "But that evening," she says, "I had to go to night school. My friend picked me up, and she said, 'How are you?' and I just sat there and cried, and I told her 'Colin's lost his job. I can't believe it, after all the years he and I gave them.' I guess I cried all the way to the school."

Guilt at Feeling the Way You Do

We began this chapter with Leslie and Murray, who were upset with their partners, felt guilty about it and seemed to think their emotions were, if not downright invalid, at least seriously ill-timed and should not be expressed right at the moment because their mates were so fragile. This is a common view, and it is important for you to realize that your emotions and concerns are neither invalid nor unusual for someone in your situation.

For example, we have mentioned Ian's worry about losing their life savings if they could not make the mortgage payments on the house. "Those payments were looming closer and closer, and I was afraid that the longer Victoria was out of work, the more employers would think she'd had some kind of problem and the longer it'd be before she started bringing in some money. I am ashamed to admit it, but even though I knew she was being really aggressive in her job search, I still tried to make her feel guilty about being unemployed. I'd ask her things like, 'What are you going to put toward the house?' and so on. My whole focus was 'Get a job, get a job, get a job.' But then, in my calmer moments, I'd feel really badly about doing that to her instead of being emotionally supportive and showing her that I knew she was doing her best."

There are sensitive ways of addressing such emotions and issues, and from our observations, it is easiest if both partners are able to share their respective burdens.

We hope, however, that in presenting these emotions in a straightforward list, we have not left the impression that they come at you one behind the other in neat, predictable little packages. They do not. The best defense is to be ready for them. Here is the first of our lists of suggestions on how to do just that.

COPING

» 1. Recognize that your feelings are valid and valuable. Even anger. But remember, there is a huge difference between expressing your anger in a calm, rational way (or even a great air-clearing fight) and engaging, as so many people do, in what is called passive controlling. That is, expressing your anger by getting mad over trivialities, or by keeping your partner waiting when you are going out, or being too tired for intimacy. And so forth.

» 2. You need at least one good friend of your own, somebody you can trust with your emotions, who lets you get things out and then move on, who doesn't expect you to be consistent. If this friend is a someone whose mate has been through a firing, so much the better.

» 3. When they are fired, many people get some emotional support from companies like the one we work for, but there are as yet few programs offered to their spouses, who are also hurting. Accordingly, you may wish to find or form your own support group. Talking with or just listening to people who are in the same boat as you are can bring an enormous sense of relief and make you feel much less alone. Your place of worship or a local Y or community center might be willing to help you in this regard.

» 4. You need your own activities. These can include a job, volunteer work, hobbies or simply a night out with a special friend or two. It will help you to separate yourself from your partner's concerns and avoid getting totally caught up in what he or she is doing. In short, you need your own life strategy during this period.

» 5. *Do not* call the company and tell them off.

» 6. Similarly, you will not be doing anything for your partner's (or your) future by making critical comments about the former employer to others (beyond your trusted confidante).

» 7. You may never know exactly why your mate was let go, and this question can haunt both of you for a long time. The best tactic is to acknowledge that you'll never know for sure, and put the matter behind you. When people ask what happened, give an answer that is consistent with the answer your mate gives to this question. This means you will have to work out your response together.

» 8. The above assumes that you have decided to tell others about the dismissal. We have already mentioned the trouble and worry you can bring down on yourselves by not telling people. One couple we encountered had told absolutely no one and, in order to maintain their deception, had stopped seeing their friends! That's a dreadful mistake. If you and your mate are open about the firing, more often than not, friends will provide invaluable emotional support—and friends can be a good source of leads during the job search.

» 9. Immediately after the firing, give yourselves time to get organized. This may mean rescheduling some social engagements over the first few days (for example, you may not want to go to cocktail parties where the first question that may be asked of your mate is "What do you do for a living?"). In short, create some quiet time to think about where you are.

» 10. Clear the decks at home. As soon as possible, with your partner, tell the children as much about the crisis as they need to know. Be reassuring and give them a reason they can understand. We'll have more to say about the kids in chapter six.

» 11. Do not pick a number out of the air and say, "Oh, it should take about three months to get a new job." How do you know that? Imposing such artificial deadlines serves only to burden you with unnecessary tension as that magical date slowly draws closer. In our experience, a job search usually takes much longer than most people imagine.

» 12. Try to imagine a worst-case scenario. Ask yourself, "What will really happen if my spouse is out of work for an unconscionably long time?" Start thinking about what down-to-earth practical things you can do if that happens. At the very least, you will find yourself dealing with a devil you know, rather than vague nightmares.

» 13. Understand that part of the reason for the shock and disbelief which follow dismissal is that most people don't expect it to happen to them. When it does and they have joined the club, so to speak, they are often astonished to discover just how large the membership is, with the most unlikely people piping up and saying, "Oh yeah, that happened to me, too."

» 14. Remember these important facts: In today's continually changing business environment, people can no longer expect to stay at one company throughout their entire working lives. Some three million professionals, managers and executives are let go in North America every year and these numbers may well increase as organizations continue to alter their structures to remain competitive. Families who cope best with job loss are those who expect change and are flexible and creative in their responses to it.

» 15. Finally, try to remember that although it may often seem so, this is not the end of the world. Most people find an opportunity eventually, and if all options are considered thoughtfully, you, your partner and your family could even end up better off than you were before.

Chapter Two

Living in Limbo

When people lose their jobs, the predictability of many aspects of their spouses' lives is threatened or simply disappears. Income, daily routines, social stature, relationships with their mates' colleagues, interactions with friends and family, where they live, their own careers, community involvement, their children's activities and education, plans for the future, the character of their relationships with their partners, and even their own sense of identity are all subject to change.

Suddenly their lives enter a holding pattern—the indefinite period of anxieties, frustration and uncertainty that we call Limbo. At the root of their anxiety and uncertainty are two primary preoccupations. The first is a serious and continuing concern about money. The second is the possibility of being uprooted, either by a move to a different neighborhood or a root-wrenching move to a new town or, perhaps, even a different country. And spouses are fundamentally helpless. They can't solve the basic problem—they can't find their mates another job.

First it's necessary to understand that such concerns can crop up in an almost infinite number of ways, depending on the circumstances and the nature of the people involved, both as individuals and as couples. For Limbo has a way of throwing light on, disrupting and often even redefining the very assumptions upon which marriages are based. For example, few people have probably ever considered that one of the basic components of the format and rhythm of most marriages is that one or both partners will be out of the house for at least ten or eleven hours every weekday. What happens when your partner is suddenly around the house more than he or she has ever been before? How do you deal with that?

Listen to Maria, a retired collections supervisor: "You can't get your cleaning done. You can't get your laundry done. I seem to be making tea five or six times a day, or have to get lunch because he's there. Ordinarily I don't bother with lunch, or I just grab a piece of cheese and run. I like to get my work done first thing in the morning and have the afternoon to myself, but I can't do that with him around. He's turned the guest room into an office, which he needs, of course, but my sewing machine lives in there and I don't get a chance to use it now. And I don't feel free to sit and talk to my friends on the phone. It's gotten to the point where it doesn't take much to start a real argument."

Maria is a homemaker whose children have grown and moved out. Sharon is a homemaker with two relatively young children: "Suddenly they have to cope with Daddy still being there at 8:30 in the morning, and he's butting in with suggestions about what they should be doing to get out the door faster, and they don't really appreciate that, because we've had our routines over the years. You don't want to hurt his feelings. He's feeling quite unsure of himself, but he's not needed at home, and there you are, his wife, wondering if you should blow your stack, because it's not just first thing in the morning. I've developed my routines, too, and his carping and suggestions go on all day."

Kevin is a self-employed insurance broker, who works from his home. Until recently, his wife, Irene, was an up-and-coming underwriter at an insurance company. When her boss was transferred to another branch, the two top candidates to fill the vacancy were Irene and a colleague. Irene had never made a secret of the fact that she regarded this person as a fool. Nevertheless, the fellow —firmly entrenched in the company's old boys' network—got the job, and the powers-that-be decided that Irene would have trouble working for her former colleague and fired her.

In vivid contrast to Kevin's laid-back style, Irene is a dynamo. "There was no way her job search was going to take every minute of her time," Kevin told us. "And since she knew the field, it was only logical that she help me with my work. I envisioned it as a partnership, but it became a dictatorship. She did everything she could to reorganize my business and my personal routines. I don't have a nine-to-five job. Often I'm out seeing people early in the morning or late at night, but if she saw me munching a sandwich and reading the paper at three in the afternoon, she'd be on my back about not working. And it didn't stop with me. She disrupted the nanny's routines. In fact, the nanny almost quit twice, and our eldest daughter was upset, because Irene got hooked on this soap and wouldn't let her watch *Sesame Street*, which was on at the same time."

Even if spouses aren't at home all day, it doesn't mean they won't experience similar problems. Karen, the sociologist, told us that when she comes home from work, her husband invariably asks if she would like him to help her get their dinner. She resents this enormously, because she thinks he should know enough to do it without waiting to be asked. "You feel a little bit hurt," Karen says. "He's home, so why can't he start dinner before I get there? If I was home all day, I would really try to make the other person appreciate what I was doing. I wish all this was over so we could talk about it."

When we met Muriel, an economist and mother of a teenage girl, her husband had been out of work for a year, and there was two months of his severance pay left. He had been fired after a fight with his boss, which had not surprised Muriel a bit. "He's around the house too much. He picks on me about my housework," she told us. "He complains about the dog. It depends on his mood. It isn't too bad if I'm feeling okay, but sometimes I'm not and I have trouble excusing him. He's angry with himself and I'm very confused. I don't know if what I'm doing for him is right or wrong. I keep asking myself if I should leave him, because I cannot take the anger and I cannot accept the silence and the depression."

We don't mean to frighten you. In all fairness, we also met many career people and homemakers who enjoyed having their partners at home for a while. One busy advertising executive even told us she was getting rather used to having a househusband, who had the place clean and dinner cooking every night when she got home. For some couples Limbo is a time and opportunity for them to correct imbalances in their relationships. But, as the experiences of Kevin, Karen and other spouses indicate, Limbo can also be a time when previous flaws in a couple's communication patterns are exaggerated and new or dormant ones are brought to light.

Many couples liken their passage through this period to walking through a mine field. Among the people we met, the trip lasted anywhere from a few weeks to two years, depending on the length of the job search and the duration of the recovery period after their mates had found new jobs. Remember, for most people, Limbo begins when their mates tell them they have been fired. But there is also a fairly large number of spouses who learn about the impending dismissal weeks, sometimes months, in advance. For them Limbo begins immediately, and they, in effect, get a double dose of it.

Before the Axe Falls

Advance warning of a dismissal can be an advantage, in that it may allow you to get over the initial shock while your partner is still employed and no major changes have yet occurred. It may also give your partner time to reassess career options and to develop concrete job search plans. If circumstances allow, he or she might even begin looking for another job before the termination date.

More commonly, though, advance warning merely generates fear and anxiety and hurtles the whole family into a state of Limbo, waiting for the firing to become a reality. As a result, even if spouses have been officially informed of their mates' impending dismissals, or have read the writing on the wall (correctly interpreting news of reorganization or a merger, or picking up hints that their mates are no longer the good corporate fits they once were), they still cannot do anything to alter the situation. This was true even in the cases of Cynthia and Kate, who viewed their spouses' dismissals from a vantage point that is given to very few people. Their stories are valuable both as examples of how pervasive

Limbo can be and as glimpses of how things are done in business today.

Cynthia's story

Cynthia and her husband, Lloyd, worked in the upper levels of a large pharmaceutical firm. His area had recently been reorganized, and one day, quite by accident, she discovered that he was going to be let go. This was not only a shock, but a terrible moral dilemma, because there was no way she should have seen that information. She kept the news to herself for two full weeks, debating whether she should betray the firm's confidence and worrying about Lloyd and their finances. She even found herself doubting Lloyd's abilities, although she knew his performance ratings were excellent. In short, Cynthia was in the unique position of entering Limbo before her husband knew he was fired. "That was pure stress," she says. "My life was on the line."

When she finally told Lloyd, she relaxed somewhat. But the firm did not break the news to him for several months, and she and Lloyd went through a long period of Limbo in which they reviewed their options. At one point, they even considered starting their own business, which would probably have meant selling their house to raise the money. In the end she stayed with the company and Lloyd decided to give consulting a try. By the time he was fired he had already lined up two good contracts.

Everything seems to have worked out well for them. Even though she has no major financial worries, and she has every faith in Lloyd's abilities, Cynthia still can't help worrying sometimes about the basic insecurity of a consultant's work.

Thus, on the home front, her Limbo really isn't over yet. And at work, she has been left in a kind of corporate Limbo, because it was her superiors who decided to fire Lloyd. As she explains it: "They're people I once looked up to for direction and guidance. A lot of that's gone now because of what I saw and the way the whole process was handled."

Kate's story

Kate and her husband, Tim, worked in the sales end of a giant manufacturer of farm machinery, often spending up to seventy percent of their time on the road. They had in fact met at work, and had been married a little over a year when the firm was sold.

At the time, they were in the same department and equally aware that it was about to be drastically reorganized, and probably not for the better. Kate was junior enough to get herself transferred to another department. "I could still make a lateral move," she explains, "but Tim's next move had to be up, and they had nowhere to put him."

Even so, Tim was assured that he would be compensated. But he soon realized that things were not right. For example, there was a dreadful uproar over some business he lost. Losing business is a common and usually temporary occurrence in that sector of the industry, and normally no one gets too excited about it. Tim's bosses, however, were furious. Moreover, he suddenly began to be excluded from meetings. The writing was on the wall.

Because of her special vantage point, Kate knew exactly what was happening to her husband. "You see," she says, "the new owners were fed up with our company losing money. They'd already booted a lot of people out of the head office and now they were starting on sales, which was run by a lot of old-school sales types. A slap on the back, let's go out for lunch and a game of golf, and the sale's done. But that's changing. Things are so tight now, and the money's just not there for that kind of thing and people don't have time to go out for a game of golf. So all these old-school types were panicking and scrambling around and trying to save their skins." And Tim, she felt, was being set up as a scapegoat.

However, Kate's special knowledge did not save her from the stresses and impulses of Limbo. As many people do, she tried to avoid the problem, and the fact that she was on the road so much gave her a ready-made excuse: "It was so easy to say, 'Well, I'm gone for two weeks, so I'll worry about that when I get back.' " But when she and Tim were home, she adds, he was very moody. "We had a very hard time as a couple. We had been a good corporate couple. We used to be in the office from 7:30 in the morning to 7:30 at night. Then we started going in at 8:30, then 9:45 and we'd be gone by 5:30. We were trying to increase our life outside the office, doing things to take his mind off what was going on because we weren't sure how to approach what was going on, and we were still having trouble as a couple." Then Kate got another, better, job in a nearby city.

Her main reason for taking it was that with all the traveling they did, she and Tim had never really spent much time together, and she figured that if she didn't always have a plane to catch, she would have time to help him and their relationship. It did not work out that way. She tried commuting to her new job, but that meant an exhausting two-hour drive each way, and she was soon coming home only on weekends.

"So it was a tough time for Tim," Kate says, "because I wasn't even around when things got really bad for him at work. I felt guilty that I had this exciting new challenge in front of me and he had a hell of a thing to deal with, and the fact that it was all happening with me out of town, as well." As if things were not bad enough, she soon found herself in a nasty personality conflict with a senior member of her new firm. She wanted to tell Tim about it, but felt she couldn't: "I didn't want to dump it on him, because he had enough to cope with. So while it was an exciting time for me, it was also a time when I really needed him but didn't feel I could come to him. And on top of everything else, I found out I was pregnant and felt I couldn't tell him about that, either. So between the two of us, when he phoned and said he'd finally been fired, we weren't ready to cope with anything and we both just fell apart."

The points to be made here are that advance warning of a dismissal is not always a blessing. We noted in the last chapter that the actual firing can bring a great sense of relief, that does not always happen. Nor does this relief mean that those who are lucky enough to experience it are also going to avoid the journey through Limbo.

For example, in the last chapter we mentioned the great relief Jennifer and her husband felt when he was fired. But she also told us that the previous six months had been very difficult, because "Stewart was extremely preoccupied with everything that was happening at the office, so at home he would be at home, but he wasn't really there. I don't think I noticed it much at first because my father died. Then my mother came for Christmas, and I honestly didn't notice. I mean, I did realize by then that Stewart was under a lot of stress, but I thought it was because of all the other things that were going on and he was stressed at having my mother around, because having my mother is stressful."

Which is a very good illustration of another important point to be made about Limbo: just because your spouse gets fired and your life seems to have been put on hold, it doesn't mean other life events and crises will hold off until a new job is found. It all seems to happen at once. To take one more example from Jennifer, the day after Stewart was fired, she had to leave for a service club convention in another city: "There just wasn't anyone I could get to go in my place on such short notice. Of course Stewart wanted me to go, but I think that after I went he wasn't so happy he'd encouraged me. And while I was away, I worried about how he was coping. It was the first time he'd ever been fired. Of course the reason was the downsizing of the company, but it still makes you wonder why it was him and not someone else who was let go. So I was worried about that, and I'd left him at home with two teenagers, who at the best of times aren't the most understanding people in the world."

Furthermore, despite personal variations, Jennifer's reaction to the advance warning she got is an example of one of the three basic ways that spouses deal with the prospect of a dismissal.

The three are:

> • 1. Ignore the signs. In the first chapter, we saw how Cheryl disregarded the possible consequences of her husband's restlessness; how Murray ignored the implications of his wife's dislike of the new president; and how, despite his wife's warnings, Carl was still emotionally unprepared for Shannon's dismissal.
>
> • 2. Accept the possibility and wait, which is what Jennifer and Kate and their husbands did in their different ways.
>
> • 3. Accept the possibility and try to do something about it, which is what Cynthia and Lloyd did, first considering a business of their own, then opting for his consulting practice.

After the Fall

The Money Squeeze

It's quite simple: job loss means your partner's income has stopped. There is probably some severance pay, but most people realize that if their mate doesn't get another job, that money will be gone, as well, no matter how much it was. Since no one can predict how long the job search will last, most spouses cannot help worrying about how long their financial resources will hold out. This uncertainty is at once a cause of considerable anxiety and one of the reasons for the Limbo that almost everyone experiences.

Bob's anxieties stemmed from the fact that, not only had his wife lost her job, his contract with the steel company was about to expire. He found himself trying to remain optimistic about their future, because he did have a lot of faith in Estelle's abilities, but he was also considering the options available if it took them a while to find work. "We have our retirement funds, and we can use them if we need to," he said. "But it's taken us a long time to accumulate that money and I'd hate to have to start all over again."

However, it's not only a matter of cash. When a job is lost, a number of benefits go, too. For example, we've already seen how quickly Angela missed the company car her husband drove. Rosemary told us she was very pleased that shortly before her husband's firing she got a job as a clerk for an importing company. This meant there was still a paycheck coming in and she and her family was still covered by a dental plan.

Rosemary has a master's degree she has never used, having by her own choice spent the last fifteen years as a homemaker. Until his firm's sudden downsizing, her husband was a well-placed mining company manager. Her job is not a permanent solution to their problem. As she put it, "You can't afford to eat and clothe your kids on one income, unless it's astronomical." With this in mind, she added, "Reg is fifty-two years old and I'm not sure how employable he is. I'm probably more employable, but not at the kind of salary he's been getting."

Gabriella has no doubt that her husband, another victim of a downsizing, is eminently employable, but she is still prey to money anxieties. "The worst part," she says, "is there is nothing I can specifically do for Jason. I can encourage him and try to be supportive at home, but I can't always manage that, because these jobs come up and even before he goes to the interview, he'll say, 'I don't want it.' I know he shouldn't try for a position he doesn't want, but with three kids to support, it's always in the back of your mind, and I keep thinking, 'Please don't tell me you don't want a job before you've even gone for the interview.'"

Gabriella is a resourceful, fundamentally positive person. But she is now in Limbo, where uncertainty, anxiety and all manner of forebodings can take on a life of their own and completely override your intellect. Thus, a dramatically reduced family income is not a problem she can always view as objectively as she might wish.

"As a result," Gabriella says, "I don't always feel as supportive as I'd like to be. Sometimes I feel, 'Oh, I wish it would all be over and he'd get on with it, take a job and be back at work so we knew where we were.' I'm making November a critical month for the job search, and that's only another four weeks away. If we haven't got something special by then, I will be a lot more worried about the future, because his financial package runs only until January and I don't think anybody looking for someone like him will be doing much hiring in December."

We've already mentioned how unwise it is to create unnecessary tension by imposing artificial deadlines on yourself. In Gabriella's case, it was especially imprudent because, as she told us in almost the same breath, the January cutoff point wasn't that at all. Jason would then receive a large lump-sum payment that could last for a good part of the following year. But fears such as Gabriella's are extremely hard to contain, even when you know you're being irrational.

In Gabriella's remarks we also saw a glimmer of one of the more treacherous side effects of financial insecurity. That is, some people come to look upon the solution to the problem, or lack of same, purely as a function of their mates' strengths and weaknesses. In extreme cases, the mate's strengths are forgotten and his or her weaknesses, both real and imagined, become the primary consideration.

Angie is a good example. Her fears about her current and future financial situation were almost completely out of control. As she described them to us: "We need a roof. We may not be able to afford it. There are all these things that come up and you just sort of think, 'Everything's on hold.' And I think, 'Okay, I won't spend. I'll save. Save really madly right now, just in case.' I'm afraid to say that to Greg, because it sounds as if I don't have any confidence in him at all, so I just sort of say it to myself. I don't buy clothes anymore. I don't buy anything. Which is a shame, because it was sort of nice before when I worked part time and I could spend my money on what I wanted."

The heart of her dilemma is that after a long career with a utility company, her husband is now looking for a job in a different industry, and Angie finds it hard to believe he has what it takes: "Greg says I'm a pessimist, but I think I tend to be a lot more realistic. I'm so upset and frightened about his prospects, because he's been in that one environment for twenty-five years and he doesn't have a lot of experience elsewhere. I mean, sure, he's capable and smart enough, but he's lacking in broader business experience, and that really frightens me, because I know there's not a lot for him out there in other fields."

Actually, Angie doesn't know. At least, she doesn't know for sure, but, both literally and figuratively, she's worried about the roof over her head. All spouses worry about it to varying degrees, but of all those we met, only one came face to face with the prospect of immediate destitution. That was Elaine, whose husband, James, suffered from a severe depression after he was fired from his job as a chief financial officer. At the time he was fifty-three, and it was his second serious depression.

"I really did worry and wonder if he would ever come back and if I'd ever have a wage earner again," Elaine says. "And he was begging me to sell the house. He said, 'You've got to do it. We've got nothing in the bank.' And I said, 'No, we can't, because it's our only asset. We have a very small mortgage, and when you want to start again, without that house the banks aren't going to lend you any money.' It was probably the smartest thing I ever did for him. We almost did hit rock bottom. I had some money of my own and I spent it all. I didn't mind, because I didn't spend it wildly, but it was truly horrendous when I looked and realized I had no more."

Although James had recovered and (financed by a second mortgage on their house) was building a successful consulting practice, the horror was still very much in Elaine's mind. For her the journey through Limbo had taken her not only uncomfortably close to the brink of poverty, but also face to face with the other great dread that looms when someone's mate loses a job—the prospect of losing your home.

After the Fall

Will We Have To Move?

Losing a home is so much more than the loss of accommodation. It is a loss of history, comfort, safety and dreams. In most cases a house is also a family's biggest asset. Along with the enjoyment in buying, furnishing and decorating it, years of scrimping, saving and sacrificing have gone into it. A home is a family's base, the center of its world, and the mere prospect of having to leave it generates an uproar of uncertainties and is the very essence of Limbo.

Basically, a couple can be forced to abandon their house for three reasons. The first is that they simply can no longer afford to live there. Second, their money is running out and they need cash to live on and finance the continuing job search. And third, the fired spouse has found a new job in another city.

This third reason has become an increasingly complex issue. Until not too long ago, it was a very simple one: it was assumed that women's careers were not as important as their spouses' jobs. Thus, women were expected to drop everything and follow their mates, no matter where the jobs took them. The notion of a man giving up his job if his wife was offered work in another city was all but unheard of. Today, women's careers are recognized as important sources of both personal satisfaction and income. Therefore, more and more men are having to face the possibility of a move if their spouses are offered jobs elsewhere.

Carol Ann was plagued by all three reasons for having to give up a home, because the most likely jobs Colin was applying for were out of town. When he lost his position at the pipe company, much of the money they had been counting on having was suddenly gone: "His pension would have been based on his best five years, and he never had his best five years. We have a nice house. We love it, but we don't know whether we're going to be able to afford to live there because it's very expensive to live in this city. We're lucky we have a cottage. If it comes to that, he can retire and we can go and live there. But if we do, I'm going to have to leave my job, which I really enjoy, and my parents are here. They're elderly and not very well, and we might have to leave them. And what if we did move to the cottage and something happened to Colin? What am I going to do, buried in the country? We use wood for heating out there. Who's going to chop the wood?"

It's no exaggeration to say that a move would uproot virtually everything that makes Carol Ann's life meaningful, and a lot of her pain flows from the sheer economic injustice of her situation. By and large, though, in situations where a move seems a possibility not because of financial hardship, but rather the location of their mates' new jobs, the people we spoke to tended to come to terms with it much more readily.

We're not saying it's ever easy, as the story of Murray and Adele illustrates. She's an artificial intelligence researcher. He's a stockbroker. Her job search resulted in an offer of a position at a distant university, which in effect acknowledged her as one of the very top people in her field. There was no way she could turn the job down. But Murray not only had a substantial network of clients in the city where they lived, he had built much of their home with his own hands. The mere prospect of a move was extremely traumatic for him, and the conflict nearly destroyed their marriage. At one point, they even considered turning it into a long-distance relationship. But Murray eventually gritted his teeth and made the move with Adele. A modem, the telephone and airplanes enabled him to keep up with the action in their former city, and he was surprised to find a number of agreeable houses for sale in their new location.

To Maria, the possibility of a move was not so much a trauma as yet another dimension to the turmoil that Limbo had imposed upon her life: "I don't want to move out of town, but if we have to, I'll go. I've resigned myself—actually, I haven't resigned myself, but I've talked myself into thinking it could be an adventure. But the thing that's really bothering us now is our mortgage is up for renewal in January, and if Howard is not working, I don't know whether there will be a renewal. It's not a very big mortgage, and my son-in-law says if we have to sell, we'll have no trouble doing that. But it's going to be an upheaval one way or another, and I'd like to be able to decide about the renewal myself and not have the bank make the decision. You really can't plan anything, not even Christmas, because he could get a job out of town and we could be in the process of packing up or he might be still unemployed."

And Gabriella, for all her fears and uncertainty, proved to be a typical member of a rather hardy group of men and women we noticed over the course of our interviews. These are people who have been through Limbo before, either because of a previous job loss or by virtue of the fact that they and their partners had packed up and moved here from other countries. In Gabriella's case, it was both, and she actually wanted to move.

"Though not necessarily to another city," she added, "but we need more space, though that obviously has to go on hold till we know where Jason is working and what income we'll have. But I think we're both confident that at some stage of the not too distant future, he'll be working again. When we emigrated twelve years ago, there was just the two of us. We didn't have jobs. We were just newly married and we decided to emigrate and see what would happen and things fell into place for us. I'm sure they will again."

My Job's Important, Too

In many ways, Gabriella is lucky. She's a free-lance computer programmer. She has a skill that is almost always in demand, and thus she can do as much as she wants, when she wants, and work at home. Accordingly, if Jason's job results in a move, even to another city, it will not greatly disrupt this aspect of her life.

Carol Ann, on the other hand, like most people, does not work at home, and a major move would mean putting a key part of her life behind her. As she explained it: "I'm a nurse. I work in a pediatrics unit. It's a gorgeous job, and I love it. I'm planning, or hoping, to do it for a lot more years, but now I don't know whether I can."

Without question, after money worries and the prospect of having to move, the possibility of having to give up or otherwise alter your relationship with your work is the greatest uncertainty that Limbo can inflict upon you.

In the case of career people, who have worked hard to gain credibility in their professions, achieved a certain level of seniority and established a network of business relationships, a move out of town as a result of a partner's job loss can be devastating. As in the case of Murray the stockbroker, the mere possibility of this happening can create terrible conflict within the people themselves and within their families. Imagine the ambivalence such spouses must feel as they watch their partners' efforts to find a suitable position where they live come to naught.

Couples may even have to decide whose career takes precedence; and even if the spouses' careers are not as prestigious or financially rewarding as their partners' jobs, they may derive as much meaning and satisfaction from their work as their mates do. So how do couples decide whose career is more important?

This question must be faced, even if a move is only a possibility. Until it is answered, the spouse's career may be put on hold, for career planning is almost impossible when so many aspects of the couple's life are in transition. Similarly, people doing part-time work or involved in community activities may be reluctant to assume any new responsibilities until they know whether they will be able to complete them.

In the previous chapter we mentioned spouses who also become quite self-conscious about their jobs, suddenly reluctant to talk about their work for fear of demoralizing their partners. Kate and Ian were two of these. So was Karen. Not only was she reluctant to talk to her husband, she also found herself becoming less adventurous. "At one time, I was always looking for new challenges," she told us, "but now I feel I should stay put, and it hurts. Like about six months ago, I had an offer. It was a risky kind of job, with some traveling, but it would have been a challenge. I told Gil I'd really like to go for it, and he said I'd better not because one of us has to be here on time for the kids, and he didn't know if he'd be able to do that once he'd found a job. So I didn't try for it. I wish I had. I wish I'd given it my best shot, and that's always in the back of my mind now."

There are no universal rules here. We also met dozens of people who spoke of the pride and pleasure they felt at being able to contribute financially at this time. They told us that their partners enjoyed hearing about their work and found their stories and problems a distraction from their own concerns; and these people further found that their work helped to balance and ease the burden of the stresses caused by their spouses' dismissal.

One of the cheeriest was Sue Ann, a theatrical agent, who positively liked being the breadwinner: "I get a kick out of it," she said, "because he made so much money before that mine never meant anything. Now I actually give him some of my salary. I'm still doing the same things with my money, but I'm a little more careful with it, and in a way it's kind of neat, because I give him an allowance every two weeks. He gets a little kick out of it because I think he can see how, in a way, it makes me feel a little more important."

A similarly positive story comes from Pat, whom we mentioned in the previous chapter as an example of how powerless a homemaker can feel. She ultimately reacted by thinking hard about her situation and decided to act. "I went back to school," she says. "I'd thought about it before, but I probably wouldn't have done it this early if this hadn't happened to Mark. But I had to do something constructive for our family, and I think that was a good thing for me. I don't have any family in the city, and my kids were still quite little. So I was really very stretched, keeping the house going, managing with the kids and going to school full time. I mean, Mark is well qualified and I knew he would never let us starve. He'd dig ditches or something. But I think rather than staying home and stewing and being anxious about him and conveying that anxiety to him, it was good for me and the family that I was out keeping busy. Ideally I would have done a master's in history. My B.A. was in history and I love it, but I wanted something that would give me a marketable skill, so I'm studying physiotherapy."

We could cite many parallel stories. But before closing this section, we must comment on a special situation still quite common among the wives of senior executives. Being Mrs. Executive is their career. As such, they expect and are expected to entertain their husbands' clients and associates; to be charming and gracious at company events; to carry themselves at all times with a dignity that reflects well upon their mates and the company; and to give the company a beneficent public presence by being active and visible in community organizations.

Thus, when her husband loses his job, such a woman may suffer an identity crisis and find herself in what we call Social Limbo. If she is no longer Mrs. Executive, who is she? What is her role? Her very identity is in Limbo until her mate finds a new job. And although this is a very painful time for her, the community expects her to continue to conduct herself with the same dignity and control she has always displayed.

In this situation, some women feel they should resign from the boards of their volunteer groups because they no longer share the prestige of their mates' former positions and therefore believe they are no longer valuable to the organization. In some cases, their resignations will be accepted, but for the most part, their contributions will have come to be valued independently of their husbands' status.

Of course, some friends will shy away from them at this time, and social invitations may dwindle. On the other hand, couples can become supersensitive to their friends' behavior, not realizing that people who don't call them right away may be doing so simply out of sympathy and concern for their privacy. However, there is no doubt about it, one of the most interesting things about job loss is that you certainly find out who your friends are.

What People Do

So far we've concentrated on Limbo's Big Three concerns: money, home and work. But as Murray so succinctly put it, "It's like everything is on hold now." Thus, not only are major plans and activities set aside for a while, or at least reassessed, job seekers' spouses also tend to put themselves on hold. That is, they have a tendency to pull in, which is how we describe the various means by which people attempt to conserve their strength and emotional resources.

Leslie described it this way: "You really don't know what you are doing. I can equate it with having experienced a death in the family, because something takes over and you just go through the motions. You're really not functioning mentally. If you can't cope with something at the time, you just put it at the back of your mind because you feel you can only cope with so much at once. 'Overload' is the word I use. I didn't write letters because I couldn't write letters. I didn't send birthday cards. I could deal with my job. I could deal to some degree with Paul's situation and the children, and that's all. Things in the house just had to go."

In short, pulling in is a survival tactic, an effort to maintain as much normalcy as possible without going off your rocker. It has an infinite number of variations. Murray, for example, told us about this somewhat typical pulling in on the part of himself and Adele: "Her firm was bought just before the start of the baseball season. We'd always looked forward to opening day and seeing all the other season's ticket holders in our section, but this year we didn't go. We were so engrossed in our own problems and had so much to talk about that chatting with other people was becoming a strain. For the same reason, we stopped going to our favorite restaurants, because the waiters and owners all knew us and would expect us to chat with them and we needed to be able to discuss things without interruptions."

We could cite many more examples; and perhaps we should, because every couple and every relationship is different. However, for that very reason, we would like to end this chapter not by trying to wrap Limbo up in a neat little theoretical package (which would be extremely difficult, given the widespread differences just mentioned), but rather by letting a few more people tell you about what living in Limbo is like in a more general way.

Murray

Describing a common dilemma: "For the first time in eleven years, my mother offered to take care of the kids. The idea was Adele and I might pop down to Atlantic City for a few days, which we've always enjoyed and done whenever we could. We both sure needed some time away, but we said no thanks. We were too wound up to go anywhere, and we were afraid to leave the city because a job opportunity might come up. It was like if we turned our backs for even a weekend, the situation would get even more out of control than it seemed to be already."

Mary Beth

Commenting on a long delay in the start of her husband's job search: "The fact that I am working was a great help. It probably would've been totally different if I was at home and we were getting on each other's nerves all day. But it is always in the back of my mind, and I'm getting impatient. Not because he doesn't have a job, but because he doesn't seem to know what he wants."

Sheila

"I felt I was on a roller coaster, because when he went for an interview with a company I really liked, I was all up and confident, and when he got rejected I was miserable. I got really high when he applied at the airline. We both enjoy traveling and I thought of all the advantages and benefits he could get, but the job went to somebody within the organization. And I thought the plastics company, where he eventually did get a job, was not very exciting at all. I mean the product they make, not the job he applied for. I was looking at each prospect from a completely selfish point of view."

Stephanie

"He was drinking more, though not in the sense of getting up in the morning and pouring a drink. But when he came home from an interview or whatever, he'd have a drink. Then it'd be a few drinks right through the evening. I finally mentioned it to him. But I found I really had to choose my words carefully. He was in such a weak position because of the firing and the question of when he was going to get a job and all those awful rejection letters coming in, so I had to be careful how I approached it."

Linda—Part One

Her Limbo was intensified by her husband's obsessive and ultimately futile attempt to start his own business, working out of their basement: "Last fall, he bought a nice warm track suit, and it took me several days to get over it, because I thought he was snuggling in for the winter. I thought he was going to turn down the heat and go down to his little office and hibernate, and that really hurt."

Larry

He found himself in a similar boat to Linda's: "My wife has always been super-organized, so when she said she was going to turn the guest room into an office and use that as a base for her job search, I thought nothing of it. But she spent at least three weeks furnishing the place, and I began to wonder if she planned to spend the next year or two in it. It's not that she absolutely needs to find a full time job. I'm sure she'd do quite well consulting, but we had a pretty ambitious investment plan for our retirement and I had to know whether we could still afford to go that route. So that and all sorts of other things were up in the air while she was running around choosing the right desk and so on."

Molly—Part One

Commenting on the value of support groups, which she learned during two previous and infinitely more serious crises: a bout with cancer eight years earlier and her husband's struggle with alcoholism: "Through the first five years of Fred's sobriety I had to learn that just because he was feeling sorry for himself, it didn't mean I had to go down in the doldrums with him. And he had to learn to cope with me as I really am, so it's a lot easier, dealing with the crisis this time. Twelve years ago, he was around the house all day and I lost all respect for him. I went through periods of absolute hate. Whereas now, I'm almost enjoying it, because he's around more, and I know he's together, and he's actively looking for a job. His attitude is good, so it's pretty hard for mine to be bad."

Linda—Part Two

"I used to make his lunch all the time, but I stopped. He wasn't always pleasant when he was eating with us and it was an inconvenience for me. I have at least two kids for lunch and sometimes three and four because I alternate with a neighbor. Several times, when I had four kids around the table, Ben decided to join us and he criticized their manners or just said things that put a damper on the meal. And one time when my friend was over, I gave her a sandwich, and Ben came in and made some comment on why she was eating our food."

They haven't spoken for a year and a half now.

Molly—Part Two

"When Jerry, our youngest, told me his dad had said, 'I am a disappointment to the family,' I went to Fred right away and I said, 'Look, thirteen years ago, you were a disappointment to this family because we didn't understand the disease of alcoholism. This time, no one's angry, no one's scared, no one's upset. For every door that closes, another will open. You know that.' We've become very active in the church, and that's given him a lot more positive way of thinking. We don't dwell on his unemployment. We all say, 'Oh, you poor unemployed manager, you,' and we laugh, and he laughs right along with us, and he's not hurt underneath."

Karen

"I don't want to be a nagger and a pusher, but we should go through this thing together. I told him I'm feeling left out, that I want to help, and he said, 'Well, I gotta do this on my own. I'll let you know if I need you.' Today I just asked, 'How was your day yesterday?' and he said, 'Okay.' And I said, 'Well, did you go to town?' And he said, 'What do you want, a full report on what I did yesterday?' End of discussion."

Bob

His wife lost her job shortly before his contract at the steel company was due to expire: "We did a major renovation on our house last year, and there's still a lot of odds and ends to take care of. I sort of want to move forward on them, but then

I don't want to. Like you say to yourself, 'There's her severance money and we did want to finish the deck and put in the hot tub, but we can't do it.' We did want to finish the bathroom with these great country tiles we bought, but we better hold back. I have this ongoing conversation in my head, but in the end, as much as we were hoping to have the major things done by this fall, we'll put it all on hold."

COPING

» 1. If advance warning is given, your mate can prepare for the dismissal by thinking about his or her career goals, preparing an up-to-date resumé, surveying the job market and so forth. Some spouses cope with the Limbo created by advance warning by discussing their mates' career options with them. However, as we've just seen, this may require some tact.

» 2. If it seems as though your mate may have to look for work in another city, develop a list of relocation criteria for you as an individual, a career person, a spouse and a parent. If your partner does the same, the two of you can then discuss your combined priorities well in advance of any employment decisions. In fact, job seekers should be aware of their spouses' criteria and priorities before they begin approaching prospective employers. Helpful advice on this and other matters can be found in the pamphlet *Tips for Every Relocating Spouse*. Details on how to obtain a copy are in the list of suggested readings at the end of the book.

» 3. You might want to do some planning of your own, identifying your criteria for new employment and updating your own resumé.

» 4. For most couples, ensuring that their resources are sufficient to cover their fixed costs will be a priority. While this may not completely eradicate their concerns, it will lessen their insecurity to some degree and allow them to get on with the business of coping with and managing the job search. One woman told us she drew some comfort from realizing that if worse came to worst, they could rent out part of their large house.

» 5. Get your finances sorted out. Determine how long your money will last. Imagine a worst-case scenario and develop contingency plans.

» 6. It may be wise to meet with a financial consultant about the tax implications of severance arrangements and possible ways in which your resources can be stretched.

» 7. It would be redundant for us to advise you to shop even more carefully than you do now, but we'd like to point out another benefit of economizing. Sheila told us about how she made a number of seemingly pointless savings, including ironing her husband's pants instead of sending them to the cleaners. That saved all of ten dollars a week. She was very bad at it and soon gave it up, feeling rather foolish. But it was not really the money that counted here. Her attempt to save these few dollars was, above all, a symbolic contribution to the household in this time of crisis, and thus it also served as a valuable and comforting coping mechanism.

» 8. At an appropriate time, sit down with your mate and discuss any plans (for vacations, renovations and so on) that you have already made. Decide which ones can go ahead, which should go on hold and which may have to be canceled.

» 9. From the outset, it is important that, as a couple, you agree that either partner may wish to review your financial situation or any other issue several times during the job search period. This does not mean you will necessarily want to modify or debate plans you've already made. Rather, we have found that just as your partner may need to go over and over certain aspects of the termination or job search, you may need to do the same with the finances. It is a concrete way of reducing anxiety and reassuring yourself that things will be okay.

» 10. Get as much information as possible about what's involved in a job search and learn how the job market behaves. This will enable you to develop realistic expectations. A good place to start is chapter four of this book.

» 11. Depending on their ages, help your children develop an action plan for themselves. Discuss their projects and plans and which ones may go ahead, which may need to be postponed and which may not be feasible at the moment.

» 12. A good way to cope with social invitations after the dismissal is to accept those you would like to attend. You can always cancel if you want, but at least you won't be stopping your life. Tell the host or hostess about your dilemma and the difficulty you are having making definite plans. Ask if it will be too great an inconvenience if you have to cancel.

» 13. Encourage your mate to spend some spare time on his or her own areas of interest. Maggie, for instance, encouraged Doug to take sailing lessons. It was a situation where he was in control and learned something new. Moreover, it was exhausting, which gave his mind a rest. His hours on the water also provided him and Maggie with some valuable time away from each other. For similar reasons, Travis, another of the spouses we interviewed, encouraged his wife, Gillian, to accept their tennis club's request that she put in a few hours a week as an instructor.

» 14. Develop an action plan for yourself. Maintain your own work and interests. Sometimes this can be desperately necessary. For example, when we asked Muriel, the economist, how she was managing during her Limbo, she laughed and said, "Oh, my God! I took all the negatives and used them to push me. I pushed the M.B.A. I'm doing, and it's going well. My job is going well. I'm more careful about what I spend. I'm aware that I'm tired, and I don't like to take medication, so I might go to a professional or do yoga." Although she was in a much more positive situation, Clare took an assertiveness training course during her Limbo and has found that it has enhanced her role in her marriage. "It was all part of me becoming more independent," she says. "I was always the quiet one in the background, and the course made me a lot more outgoing." She and Les also made time for themselves. He worked hard at his job search four days a week and took Fridays off. She had every second Friday off and they would enjoy an outing together.

» 15. Further to the above: remember, whether it be a job, volunteer work, a hobby or other recreation or just time with a good friend, you need it. These are necessities, not luxuries.

» 16. Try to avoid what Elaine did. It took a very long time for her husband to recover from his depression and begin his consulting career. Throughout this very rough period, she constantly had to keep building up his morale and convincing herself that things were going to be all right. The strain was often unbearable, and for a while she became dependent on sleeping pills. "A big reason for that," she said, "was I didn't have anybody to share my pain with. But that was my fault, because I didn't take anyone into my confidence."

» 17. It's easy enough for us to say to communicate with your partner on all important issues, but that is often easier said than done. Only one of the many problems that can crop up here is that couples may talk around, but not about, the real issues. Angie and Greg, for instance, are always debating his optimism and her pessimism, especially her habit of constantly imagining the worst. Our impression is that the issue is not really optimism or pessimism. Rather, Angie feels angry and badly about Greg's dismissal. She is frightened for their future and needs to be able to discuss the range of options they have. At the same time, she doesn't want Greg to think she lacks faith in him, so she doesn't really discuss this. For his part, Greg knows she's feeling badly, but rather than address these issues directly, he tries to cheer her up with his optimism, which drives her crazy. They are each trying to avoid hurting the other, but their avoidance is making them feel worse.

» 18. Remember, don't be shy about telling people your mate has been fired. Murray wasn't, and he was amazed by what he found: "I didn't begin every conversation by saying 'Hey, my wife's been dumped,' but if it was appropriate, I mentioned it. One time, for instance, I happened to mention it to one of my colleagues, and she said her husband had gone through the same thing a couple of years ago and their nephew had just been mergered out of a job. I heard a lot of stories like that. It was like when you're reading a book and you see a word or a name you've never seen before and then all of sudden you're seeing and hearing it everywhere."

» 19. Finally, take a tip from Gabriella: "My uncle was forty-eight, had a heart attack and died at work. I suppose that puts it all in perspective. This isn't the worst thing that can happen to you. Sure it's bad, but no one has died, nobody is deathly ill, so you are going to get through it. It may take a long time, it may be difficult, but hopefully you've still got each other, you've still got your kids. Things will get better."

Chapter Three

What's Happening to
Your Partner?

A lot of what's happening to you flows directly from what's happening to your mate. The trouble is, if you are like most of the spouses we talked to, it's not always easy for you to know exactly what your partner is going through. People who have just been terminated may not be able to talk about their feelings very clearly. They may talk constantly, or they may be strangely quiet. Maybe their moods swing all over the emotional landscape.

Whatever the case, although you may be feeling hurt for your partner, you are probably also wondering whether the reactions to the termination that you are seeing are normal, or if your partner's feelings and ways of expressing them are a sign that he or she is having an unusually hard time coping with the event.

This chapter is to set your mind at ease. Although they may vary in duration and intensity, the emotional stages that people experience after a dismissal are fairly common, reasonably predictable and, above all, completely understandable. By understanding these stages, you will be able to accomplish two things: you will be better able to cope with your partner's different feelings, thus easing some of your own hurt and concern, and you'll be in a much better position to be as helpful to him or her as you wish to be.

First you must understand that your partner is probably very frightened. Many people have never had to search for a job before and the prospect of having to do so now is quite alarming. It is essential for you to understand what it means for people to lose their jobs in the first place.

At its most basic, their jobs were a place to go every day. They enjoyed a certain position within their firms and an almost familial relationship with colleagues and staff. They had challenging problems to engage their minds and opportunities for achievement and recognition.

Listen to Carol Ann describe her husband's relationship with the pipe plant: "He once actually told me, 'Pipe gets under your skin.' I laughed, but I could see what he really meant was the plant. He knew every bit of raw material that went in one end and every inch of pipe that went out the other. He knew every one of those two hundred people's names. In the early days, I don't know how many times he was called to work in the middle of the night because something was wrong. He always cursed and complained, but I could tell he wouldn't have had it any other way."

Besides providing a sense of place within a special community, work provides people with income and, thus, the security of knowing they can provide for their families. In short, work forms a crucial portion of a person's identity, and losing it is, understandably, devastating.

Angela related just how catastrophic a job loss can seem. After a night of tears, she and Percy got on with the business of coping. But this was his second dismissal in two years, and he was handling it fairly well. "The first dismissal," Angela told us, "was an entirely different story. He was let go on a Monday. He had a beaten look about him, but he seemed to be coping all right. Then on the Thursday, we were having dinner and Percy got up from the table and went down to the basement. I knew something was wrong, because you can't go through this without some sort of reaction, no matter how strong you are. So I followed him, and I'll never forget what I saw for the rest of my life. He had cracked. He had broken down. He had just come to the full realization of what had happened, and he was crying. These huge, awful sobs. He couldn't even speak. All I could do was be there."

Percy was not nearly as keen about his work as Carol Ann's husband was about his, but it still meant an awful lot to him, probably more than he realized until he was fired. Even people who actually dislike their jobs can sorely miss them when they are fired.

The Reactions

One of the most common reactions to a dismissal is shock. It may come before the actual termination if it is learned that the company is about to downsize or is involved in a takeover or a merger.

For some, denial is a way to sublimate the agony. This defensive posture can last until the shock of the actual firing. Even when an employee does face the facts squarely and starts the job search, the firing can still be a shock when it happens.

However, shock and denial most frequently occur after a dismissal, and among the hardest hit are employees who have recently had excellent performance reviews or have been given raises. Only two weeks before he was fired, Maggie's husband, Doug, was given a bonus of fifty thousand dollars, which made his termination all but incomprehensible. "It was like his world had been chopped in half," Maggie says. "On the one hand, there was all the money they had given him, presumably because he deserved it, and on the other, they didn't want him any more. It didn't make a bit of sense."

It is understandable, then, that shock often manifests itself as numbness or confusion, which can last for hours, or even days, in the form of disbelief and disorientation. However, there are people who completely lose their sense of reality as the result of a dismissal. One such person is Mac, a gentle, kindly guy, whose job in a rapidly expanding retail organization had outgrown his abilities. He seemed to not understand that he had been fired and kept going back to sit in his old office, visit with his former colleagues and try to give them a hand. Maybe the fact that a replacement for him had not yet been found and the office was still empty encouraged his belief that he hadn't been fired after all. The company finally had to lock his office. He still didn't get the message, and for weeks after, he refused to accept the written confirmation of his dismissal that the company sent to him via courier.

But shock and disbelief are only part of the story. Two more emotions that people commonly feel are intense anger and bitterness, which arise for numerous, often overlapping, reasons:

- **The decision to leave the company was taken out of their hands.** As one woman explained it, "I thought I was indispensable because I was good at my job. I knew I'd move on someday, but I always thought it would be at my own initiative."

- **A sense of injustice.** People who have given the best years of their professional lives to a company can't help but feel angry and bitter. Later we will be looking at the marital troubles of a couple named Sharon and Ted. At the root of their strife is the fact that a year or so before he was dismissed Ted's company was taken over by another. He became a key member of the transition team, which meant his work almost doubled and his family life went right out the window. However, he thought the sacrifice was worth it, because he still had a job and was an important part of the new scheme of things. He wasn't, and they fired him as soon as the transition was complete.

- **A sense of betrayal.** The anger here has similar roots to that outlined above. For instance, Kate's husband, Tim, was a good amateur hockey player and a team-oriented guy, who felt at home in his company because his superiors were always comparing the staff to a team. But when Tim lost that bit of business we mentioned earlier, his bosses turned on him. It was only natural then that he should look back to hockey for an analogy to explain his feelings about what had been done to him. As he told his wife, "If you have the skills and you practice and play hard and have a good game, you get recognized and rewarded. You don't get benched or traded for having a bad game now and then."

- **Anger at the way the dismissal was carried out.** The abruptness and lack of sensitivity with which many termination meetings are handled can rob people of their dignity and leave them feeling humiliated and bitter for years afterward.

- **Anger at the sheer senselessness of it all.** Maggie's husband was baffled by the way his large bonus was almost immediately followed by his firing.

But as well as baffled, people who have received good performance reviews and bonuses or raises before they were fired can become extremely angry, then bitter. At the root of it is shock at the wholly unexpected termination, coupled with a feeling of being hoodwinked by the company.

This happened to Harriet. In college, she studied marketing and showed a distinct aptitude for that type of work. However, after marrying Vern, she gave up her career to become a homemaker. When Vern lost his job and was unemployed for quite a while, Harriet returned to marketing, going to work at a large dairy products firm.

Within a few years, her innovativeness and organizational savvy led to her appointment as marketing manager for the company's two key products, a job that gave her an enormous amount of satisfaction. Then, about a year ago, a new management team took over and began to let people go. Harriet, however, continued to receive excellent performance reviews and was personally assured that there would always be a place for her in the company, which was a lie. She was let go hardly a month later.

"Harriet was absolutely distraught," Vern told us. "She spent a lot of time crying, saying 'Why me? What did I do wrong? Should I have done this? Should I have done that?' And galloping right alongside all this self-analysis was absolute rage and eventually just plain bitterness at being lied to and, for no reason that she could see, cheated out of her job."

There is nothing shameful or uncommon about grief and tears. They are a natural expression of the profound sense of hurt and loss and rejection that many people experience when they are dismissed.

Anger also flows from the terrible loss of income, friends, challenges, achievements, prestige and all the other things people go to work for. This is especially true if the firing thwarts their career plans and prevents them from completing projects they may have been totally involved in and very excited about. If their search for a new job is prolonged, the anger and bitterness will increase as they think back on the company and people who put them in this awful position. From our observation, most people feel some lasting bitterness, even after they are happily re-employed.

We have also observed that partners tend to balance each other's emotional reactions to a job loss. For example, if one is repressing anger, the other is often quite outspoken, expressing the rage that both of them may in fact feel.

But whether or not people who lose their jobs hide their feelings or vent them openly, the emotions generated by a dismissal can be consuming, and if intense anger persists, it can interfere with the job search.

However, not all people are upset or enraged when they've been fired. If personality conflicts, organizational changes and other factors have created an untenable working climate for them, they may be genuinely relieved to have the situation come to an end. The same applies to people who have wanted to leave in order to pursue other interests and just needed a nudge.

The people who tend to be the calmest about a firing are those who have read the signs correctly and prepared themselves for the possibility of termination. In our experience, the dreaded extreme of anger resulting in physical violence is very rare, although it and other forms of revenge may be fantasized about and uttered. Bitterness and anger are, as we have said, persistent things, but they must somehow be put into proper perspective. For example, it was Jennifer who told us about Rick's fruitless anger, and she made a point of comparing his behavior with her husband's attitude. "Rick did get a raw deal," Jennifer said, "but it's going to take him a long time to find another job, because employers just back right away from people who are very angry. My husband was bitter at times, but he didn't tell the world. He could've honestly said the people who fired him were crazy to eliminate those positions, but he didn't. It just creates a negative impression, and getting a new job has a lot to do with the image you project."

For some, the first reaction to the shock of their firing may be flight. This is a way of trying to, at least temporarily, avoid the painful reality and emotional upheaval of being released. Such people may want to leave the termination meeting quickly, even before hearing the terms of their severance package. On very rare occasions, though, withdrawal can be an attempt to deny reality altogether, and the individual, like the man who kept coming back to his office, may need some help in accepting the termination.

At the other extreme are compliance and acceptance. Some people appear to accept the firing without much difficulty or emotion. For example, Frank not only planned the downsizing of his firm, but also included his high-level position among those who were to get the axe. He, more than anyone, knew the business reasons why he should go. He fully accepted the situation and went into his job search with one of the most positive attitudes we've ever seen.

A person's initial acceptance of his or her firing could be followed by a rapid slide into anger or depression. In such circumstances, people may still fully understand their former employers' actions, but come to be upset by what these actions have meant to them and their families.

Two more common emotions are shame and embarrassment, which may surface in the first stages of the termination as the fired employee desperately wonders how to tell his or her spouse and those around them. A major reason for this is that a firing often hits people who are high achievers, and is thus perceived by them as a failure and a negation of all they have accomplished. On top of the shock and pain of the dismissal, they are also acutely embarrassed and often very reluctant to tell anyone what has happened to them. A few even consider not telling their spouses! In some cases, they may not tell anyone other than the immediate family and order them to keep it a secret.

As people do begin to tell others about their firing and find that the news is generally accepted without judgment, they may become more comfortable and their sense of shame may disappear. Some never get over their embarrassment, yet still bring themselves to tell others as needed, which is particularly important if they are to conduct an effective job search.

However, there is a noticeable number of people whose pride is so deeply wounded that it seriously interferes with their search. That is, their embarrassment keeps them from getting out and making the many contacts one needs in order to find a new job. This happened in a rather curious way to Vito, a software engineer. When he was fired, he also lost his company car. That's the usual course of events, but this was no normal company car. It was a unique foreign model, which Vito and his wife had had great fun picking out and truly loved. This automobile became the focal point of his and his wife's embarrassment about the firing. They were too ashamed to tell anyone why they no longer had their fancy car. They didn't even tell their kids.

The upshot was that Vito became so desperate to get another job and the wherewithal to replace the car that he took the first position that was offered to him. It was not the right job for him and he was fired again about six months later.

Anxiety and fear are also common reactions to termination. One of the big worries is finances, so don't be alarmed or offended if your partner suddenly wants to review household spending. He or she needs to know where you stand financially, and so do you, for that matter. Accordingly, once the severance package has been agreed to, the two of you should look into ways of making the money stretch as far as possible.

Some people panic and want to do such things as pull the kids out of their private schools and eat franks and beans every night. Others will want to maintain the appearance of normality at any cost. Still others, formerly very easygoing about spending, will now want to control every cent. Whatever the case, your partner's money worries, and your own, are very real. Thus it is best for you to sit down and discuss your finances as realistically as possible, rather than worrying separately and arguing about every expenditure.

Generally, you will want to postpone major purchases. However, a very useful investment, if you don't have one already, can be a home computer. As one woman told us, "It seemed like a lot of money at the time, but now he can do his own resumés and letters."

Another big anxiety is that some people believe they'll never be employed again. Even the most successful people may worry that they have some defect they can't see but prospective employers will spot at once. Or if an employer doesn't spot the defect and they are hired, they will fail at that job, too.

They rarely articulate such fears, but these can be manifested in a number of ways. For example, they may be reluctant to launch the job search, combining their fear of further failure with the fear that comes from not knowing how to look for a job. Or they may indeed know how to look for one and be daunted by the sheer size of the task. And they may feel trapped, fearing that they will be unable to locate job openings at their former level but be too ashamed to apply for lesser positions with lower salaries.

Conversely, their panic may make them jump at the first offer they get, regardless of how well it meets their abilities and needs.

Fear and anxiety can also arise from the sense of vulnerability that comes from feeling they are victims of circumstance. Other people decided to fire them and other people will decide whether to hire or not hire them. Thus, no matter how good they are or how hard they try, someone other than themselves will determine their fate. This feeling of vulnerability may continue into their next jobs, at least until they feel happy and reasonably successful there. And if their new positions turn out to be a bad fit, their anxieties and other discomforts will continue, especially if they are reluctant to quit and subject their families to the frustrations and insecurity of another job search.

For example, Mel hated the levels of organization that he had to negotiate every time he wanted to do anything in his job as a technical manager for a large auto parts manufacturer. When he was fired, he felt somewhat relieved to be free of the endless red tape, and told everyone he was happy to be out of there. Privately, though, he was worried about his financial situation. Jobs at his level and in his specialty were few and far between, and as his search dragged on, he became more and more panicky, and accepted the first offer he got.

However, in his eagerness for any kind of job, Mel failed to ask the executives who interviewed him a lot of important questions about the company's way of doing things. Consequently, he was not in the job a week before he realized that this firm was, if anything, wrapped in more red tape than the company he had left. The resulting stress built quickly, and his wife, Constance, watched with alarm as he grew more tense by the day. She suggested that he leave the company and look for a better position, but he wouldn't hear of it. "There's no way I'm ever going to allow us to live on the edge again" was his inevitable reply. Mel's still in that job, and he and his family remain prisoners of his fears and sense of vulnerability.

Controlling Interests

Executives, managers and professionals tend to be action-oriented people, accustomed to taking control and getting things done. At work, if they do not actually tell people what to do, they still have a certain influence on the course of events. Thus the *loss of control* that accompanies their termination is exceptionally galling and distressing, and they have two major ways of trying to compensate for it.

The first is so common, we've given it a name: "The Antique Store Syndrome." That is, wanting never again to leave their fate in someone else's hands, many people who have lost their jobs will look into the possibility of opening their own businesses. Often this is unrealistic in terms of their skills, temperament, finances and, above all, their capacity to take risks and endure the endless hours required to establish a business. However, it is important for their mates to realize that most people who consider the business option will find a certain therapeutic value in carefully examining the possibilities, if only to dismiss them. In some cases, it is their one opportunity to explore a dream, mentally test it and then release it for all time. At least it is they, and not anyone else, who has made the decision.

Sometimes, dismissal can result in the establishment of a successful new business. However, even if they have every confidence in their partners' skills, many spouses find the risks of starting a new business rather overwhelming. Take, for instance, the story of Cheryl and Glen: Glen had been faithfully applying for jobs and was at last on the brink of getting one. "But," Cheryl says, "he was doing it for me. He'd be a vice president and receive x amount of dollars and there would be profit sharing and the car and the rest of it. He thought it would make me happy. But I could see he'd be doing a lot of traveling again, and at this point, he'd been home for three months, and it had been a nice change.

"So I said, 'That's not really what you want, is it?' He said no, and I asked him what he did want and he said he wanted to start his own company."

At that point Glen didn't know what kind of company. But not long after this, a small paper-recycling plant was up for sale. Cheryl suggested that he go and look at it. When he came home, Glen announced that he was going to buy that company. "The price was ideal, but the market for that particular service was in a slump, and that's what worried me. I said I'd rather we got into something that's booming. I wanted to go to the library and do some research, but Glen said, 'I don't really care what's booming out there. Everything's cyclical.'"

Glen's instincts were right. But it was a long time before Cheryl's insecurities faded and she accepted their success and, to some degree, became resigned to her loss of the perks she'd enjoyed as the wife of a vice president of a large corporation. This brings us to the key point about any spouse's role in a mate's decision on whether to go into his or her own business. Because of the risks, expense and hours involved, a decision to start a business will have an infinitely greater effect on the spouse's life than any decision about which job to take. Therefore, the spouse should be involved from the beginning. That way, if his or her mate does decide to go ahead, the spouse, while perhaps not wholly agreeing with the decision, will at least be aware of the reasons for it and have some idea of the inevitable stresses and sacrifices that await down the road and be better equipped to cope with them.

For instance, in the last chapter we saw how Cynthia, despite her faith in Lloyd's talent, was still uneasy about the economic risks that went with consulting. One big factor in her acceptance of his decision was her awareness that the bureaucracy at the pharmaceutical firm stifled him. He was at his best creating ways to market products and implementing them, not plodding through the maze of reviews and approvals he had to endure before he could try anything new.

Olive, a homemaker, has equally strong faith in her husband. But, like Cynthia, she really can't muster complete faith in her partner's business venture. When we met Olive, Craig had just been fired from a trust company and had decided to free-lance in his rather arcane financial specialty. "He's extremely strong and he looked upon the firing as an opportunity," Olive says. "He's perhaps better at dealing with change than I am. He's definitely brighter than I am. His faith is stronger. He's a very creative guy. For me to be truly optimistic about something, I have to be one hundred percent sure in my heart. So there's this fear about the business. What happens if it doesn't go? I suppose he could always get another job, but that might not be very easy, either, considering his age and his level."

For her part, Linda is coming face to face with what Olive fears most. After his firing, her husband, Ben, spent more than a year trying to develop and sell an improvement to the just-in-time inventory systems that are in place in so many factories these days. It seemed like a brilliant idea. But part of Ben's failure to make a success of the business came from his character and limitations. As Linda puts it: "If it had caught on it would've been an enormous success, but Ben thought he could do everything himself, which was a mistake. For one thing, he's not a salesman. I don't know if he's decided to look in other directions yet or not, and what's worrying me is I don't think it's that easy to get a job when you've been out of the work force for such a long time. I don't know how employers feel when you've attempted something on your own and it hasn't worked."

Yet, for all her insecurity and the year and more of strife that went along with Ben's business efforts, Linda does not view the experience negatively: "I guess I've always had the feeling it was going to be difficult for him, and I knew it would be a long time, but I also knew how fortunate he was in being able to try his own business, and I think that really was important. I never told him to go out and get a job. I've tried to keep up a certain standard of living, a certain quality of life and not nag and talk about 'poor us.' I think we should be very grateful, because even if you fail, having the opportunity to try something on your own can be a very positive experience."

Linda and Olive can also take us into the second major area where people try to compensate for the loss of control they enjoyed at work: their homes. In the last chapter, we caught a glimpse of the disruption and bad feeling caused by Irene's efforts to take control of her husband's business, his way of working, the nanny's routine and even her daughter's TV viewing. In Olive's case, rather than making a power grab, her husband was merely thoughtless and the solution was a simple matter of logistics. "I like the house neat," she explains. "He's a slob, and I've lived with it for twenty-one years. But after he was fired, he started plunking himself down at the kitchen table with his computer. I put up with it for about a week.

"I figured, okay, he's feeling down, this is a big adjustment for him. Then I finally said, 'When I do a bit of cooking or cleaning up, I want to have some company with the radio. If the phone rings, I should be able to pick it up. I should at least have the freedom of my own kitchen.' And he looked at me and thought about it and said, 'You know, you're right,' and he took his stuff downstairs."

If only it were all that simple. Countless people told us about how, even if their partners had set themselves up in a basement office, they still made forays up to the kitchen and elsewhere and tried to exert control over them, the kids and even pets.

In such situations, most spouses intuitively understand what's going on. For example, as we indicated earlier, Ted's behavior stemmed from the fact that about a year before he was dismissed, his company had merged with another and his workload nearly doubled. "So he hadn't been around the house much," Sharon says, "and I had been forced to become very independent of him. Then all of a sudden he's home most of the day and demanding that I become dependent again."

In the same vein, Linda understood that a lot of Ben's nasty behavior came from the frustrations he was facing in his attempts to make his business idea work. But no matter how much a spouse understands that his or her partner's actions are an attempt to re-establish a sense of importance, worth and self-esteem, their empathy will often clash with their resentment, and over time, the latter will generally win out.

Resentment can continue to build. Counteracting it is usually easier said than done. However, if you are faced with such a situation, you do have an advantage in that you probably know why your partner is acting that way, while he or she does not. If you are patient and go about it delicately, this can be the foundation of a nonconfrontational negotiation of what diplomats call "spheres of influence." Something along the lines of: "Okay, if you want to be in charge of the cars and the yard, fine. But I've been handling the kitchen on my own for years, and I'd like to continue doing that." No matter how much you understand your partner's feelings, you still need to state your own needs clearly.

More Reactions

Depression is common among men and women who have lost their jobs and may be characterized by a deepening sadness, lethargy, lack of motivation and, in a very few cases, immobilization. It results from the numerous losses associated with termination, and it is a normal and usually temporary response. It does, though, appear and disappear at different stages of the job search. Carol Ann described it to us this way: "Sometimes when he's quiet and I ask, 'What are you thinking about?' he'll say, 'What do you think?' and then I know he's really low. It comes back to him in waves."

Loneliness and a sense of isolation are bound to afflict people who are engaged in a long and frustrating job search. If their families are aware of what they are going through and are appropriately supportive, these feelings will come and go fairly easily. However, if the family fails or refuses to grasp how difficult a search can be, the condition can become very painful. This was much the case with Ross and Janice, both of whom were, for a while, unemployed simultaneously. Apart from taking every opportunity to accusingly ask if he had found work yet, Ross's parents refused to discuss his job search at all, and he eventually learned that they were telling people he was still employed.

Janice's family was even more unhelpful. An accomplished director of human resources, she was looking for a job with a company that saw her as vice presidential material. Given her credentials and track record, this was not the least bit unreasonable, but her family seemed incapable of understanding what she did and what she was looking for. During one phase of her search, she had a series of meetings with the top executives of a packaging firm. On the ground floor of the building where the firm had its head office was a glove boutique. Janice's parents happened to know that the boutique needed a counter clerk, so all the while she was carrying on rather delicate negotiations with the packaging company, her family was hounding her to grab the job in the store downstairs! Luckily, Ross and Janice's support of each other counterbalanced their families' obvious lack of understanding.

Enthusiasm and optimism may be the primary mood of people who greet termination with relief and see it as a chance to find a position that is a better fit for their personalities and skills. Thus the result can be a highly motivated job search. But, optimism can also be a reflection of unrealistic expectations or a way of putting up a brave front to allay the fears of a worried spouse.

Enthusiasm and optimism may be also be hopeful reactions to a specific job opportunity and, as such, are the high end of what has been termed the elation/depression syndrome or "yo-yo" effect. These refer to the cycles of hope and dejection that accompany having made it through several interviews for an exciting job prospect and then being told, sometimes weeks later, "We've found someone who more closely meets our requirements."

With this in mind, it's easy to understand how frustrated job seekers can feel. But the inevitable impatience with the job-search process, while quite understandable, can be a rather dangerous extension of frustration, especially if the person loses sight of what jobs are right for him or her. As we saw with Mel and Vito, panicking and accepting a job that doesn't match one's skills, personality and preferences can lead only to further misery and maybe another dismissal down the road.

One of the saddest instances of this that we encountered was the case of Agnes and her husband, Earl, a traffic manager. He was not particularly devastated by his dismissal, largely because he and Agnes thought he'd find another job quickly. He did not, and after ten long months, he accepted one of three lesser positions, and it was only then that he truly began to miss his former job. For Agnes, this meant that her Limbo had really only just begun.

"When he got the job, I breathed a sigh of relief and thought my life would get back to normal again, but it hasn't," Agnes told us. "As time goes on, it gets worse, because he's still looking for another job. He's not happy there, and he's having a more difficult time now than he did when he was off work. His work was his life. He doesn't have many hobbies, but he loved going to work every day. I used to admire him so much. Now he just has negative things to say about his work, and I'm devastated by it, because I don't know how to cope with it. I could cope with him being out of a job, but I don't know how to cope with this."

It's difficult to feel good about other people when you're not feeling good about yourself. Thus another manifestation of frustration and rejection is a shorter fuse. Many people told us that their partners became more short-tempered, quicker to criticize them and their children and often less tolerant of friends and others. Sometimes it is hard to tell whether this is a control maneuver of the kind mentioned above or simple crankiness.

Guilt might also be felt by those who believe that as aggressive as they may be in their job searches, they are still not getting results. Your optimism and reassurance can go a long way at such times.

People can also become bored if an extended search fails to produce concrete results. A big reason for this is that at the start of a search there is, as we'll see in the next chapter, a tremendous amount of work to do, and they are busy all the time. Later on there will still be a lot of work to be done, but it will require considerable effort and willpower to sustain the momentum. A good way to do this is to balance the search with a hobby or some outside project. Sheila's husband, for instance, remained active in the softball league he belonged to and organized the regional championships. The key, of course, is to keep a good balance between the search and other interests.

Lack of confidence can be experienced by the most talented people. Firing is such a sharp blow to their self-esteem that many are suddenly unable to recall their skills, knowledge and achievements. It's not uncommon for them to find themselves thinking along the lines of "because someone didn't want me, I'm a loser. I must have nothing to offer." With a little help, this temporary amnesia disappears and the job seeker realizes that winners get fired, too, and that he or she is not only valuable, but indeed very marketable.

Vern nudged Harriet in that direction when the marketing director of a new health food company asked her to be a consultant. "At first she was scared," Vern said. "Getting fired from that dairy products outfit had knocked her confidence right into the basement, but I told her, 'You can do it. I know you can, so just roll up your sleeves and get in there and do the bang-up job you've always done.' She did, and that was the beginning of the restoration of her confidence."

Frustration, worry, loss of self-esteem, boredom and a host of other factors may lead to various forms of substance abuse. Rosemary, for example, told us that Reg's wine intake increased worrisomely. "He'd always had a glass at dinner, and now he was going through a bottle and a half a day, mainly because he was home being bored. Once, he sort of collapsed in the family room and all of a sudden it hit me—God, this is what alcoholism is all about, and that was hard. But I think it shocked him, too. Not that he'd admit there was a problem or anything, but he has pulled back a bit."

Finally, decreased or increased sexuality may each be manifestations of a loss of self-esteem. Decreased sexuality may be a result of depression and is one of the ways lowered self-esteem can be acted out. If sex is viewed from the standpoint of performance, rather than pleasure, the fear of failing in yet another area of one's life may prevail and become a self-fulfilling prophecy.

Increased sexuality can be an attempt to reassert one's sense of worth, which received such a severe blow from the firing. But remember: it may above all be a way to receive pleasure and comfort at a time when such good feelings are needed.

Christmas

Whatever your religion, the Christmas season may be a difficult time. Even if you resented having to go in previous years, be prepared for a sense of loss associated with not attending the office Christmas party and other functions that are part of the business world's round of hospitality and conviviality in the holiday season. If your mate's colleagues were, or are still, your friends, this feeling of loss may be particularly keen.

If you cannot meet your children's gift expectations or be as generous in giving to others as you'd like, your partner may feel a new surge of anger and disappointment at the firing. And because prospective employers' interest in holding interviews and doing other recruiting activities tends to slacken around Christmastime, the season could be doubly frustrating. On top of this, Christmas is a time when many people just feel low, and being out of work simply aggravates this. If the seasonal blahs seem to be creeping up on you and your household, you might find some comfort and advice in Jo Robinson and Jean Staeheli's thought-provoking book, *Unplug the Christmas Machine*, which discusses ways families can create some of the traditional, noncommercial holiday spirit.

Acceptance of Being in Transition

In time, most people come to accept the transition period between past and future employment.

They are rarely entirely comfortable with it, but there is a greater sense of ease and a better understanding of what needs to be done in terms of their job search. However, we should warn you that acceptance is not a constant thing. It comes and goes at various stages of the search; and we have found that if the job search extends beyond the initial estimate of its duration, a person will most likely go through a period of disappointment. This often happens around the six-month point. It's generally a temporary low, and more often than not impels job seekers to reconsider their goals.

For example, Janice had been well-prepared for her job search. In fact, she had planned the downsizing of her firm and the elimination of her position. In the past, headhunters and others had always come to her with job offers, and she was confident that she would be re-employed within three or four months. When she wasn't, and the fourth month passed, she began to panic. She had an excellent severance package, but her husband, Ross, had decided to return to school to prepare himself for a new career, and they also had two young sons and a baby to consider. Thus, at the half-year mark, Janice hit a real low. She and Ross discussed it and decided that a two-week vacation would be worth the expense. They were right. Janice came back rejuvenated and resumed her search with new vigor. Three months later, she was happily settled in a job that fit her talents and ambitions to a tee.

During such lows and the resulting reconsideration of their goals, job seekers may decide to broaden their search to include other sectors of the job market or different locations. They might also reassess their job targets and decide they were aiming too high. Then again, they might re-evaluate their previous work and decide they were in the right job, but at the wrong place. And, like Janice, they just might reconfirm that their new job targets are entirely reasonable and continue to pursue them.

Such reconsideration is not a bad thing. As you have already seen (and will continue to see throughout the book), job loss becomes a turning point in the lives of many people. Faced with the fact that the ultimate reward for their sacrifices was rejection, they become open to truly rewarding pursuits. With their spouses, they establish new goals that are consistent with new or previously ignored values, and the pursuit of these goals, coupled with this fresh awareness of what is really important, can give them and their families a fulfilling and exciting new lease on life.

COPING

On the face of it, many of the suggestions in this list might seem better addressed to your partner. However, we believe you will be in a better position to help your mate, and yourself, if you have a clear idea of some of the things he or she could be doing to cope with the emotional turmoil that follows a termination.

Before beginning the list, though, we'd like to share some words of wisdom from a couple of the spouses we met. The first is Bob. He and his wife were looking for work at the same time. He said: "We're a good team. She gives me encouragement and support without being patronizing and I do the same for her. It's a team-building exercise, so if one of us gets a job and the other doesn't for a while, or when we're both back at work, that teamwork is still going to be there for us."

Stephanie, describing her view of the spouse's role at this time: "I think just being there for them and not going off the deep end, because that's the last thing they need. Their identities have been shattered, and if you fall down with them, you could have real problems."

That is both good general advice and a succinct description of the spouse's fundamental dilemma—how do you balance your mate's needs with your own? A lot of people told us that their partners seemed so frail that they believed they could very easily destroy them. In some cases, that may be true. But after working with hundreds of people who have lost their jobs, our experience is that while most are indeed very hurt by a firing, they are also quite strong and resilient. Thus, although it's very important to be sensitive to your partner's needs (which is a good idea at any time), it's equally important to take good care of yourself and pay attention to your own needs. With that in mind, here is the list:

» 1. Act as a sounding board. Your partner may need to go over and over every detail of the day of the firing and come to his or her own explanation of why it happened. Continue listening throughout the job search, trying to truly understand what he or she is saying and empathize with it. Also pay attention to the nonverbals. Hugs and smiles help a lot.

» 2. Expect your partner to have emotional ups and downs and allow extra leeway for unusual behavior. At the same time, keep a discreet eye open for excessive drinking and other signs of serious trouble. If you spot any, try to steer your mate toward more constructive coping methods.

» 3. It is important for job seekers to have areas in their lives where they can still feel a sense of accomplishment, purpose and control, so they should be encouraged to plan activities for the times they are not engaged in the job search. Remember Sheila's husband's softball league; how Maggie encouraged Doug to take sailing lessons; and the way Travis urged Gillian to do a bit of instructing at the tennis club.

» 4. It'll be hard, but try not to personalize your partner's anger and criticism of you. Do not engage or get caught in it by responding in kind. Get out of the way until things cool down. Then, if the matter is something you should discuss, choose a time when both of you are calm.

» 5. Although you and your partner may be very angry about the firing, it's important to avoid all temptation to bad-mouth the former employer. It will only make your partner's contacts wary about referring him or her to their contacts, and prospective employers will be concerned about your mate's judgment and leery about allowing such bitterness into their organizations.

» 6. In connection with the above, it may be useful for the two of you to come up with a non-negative reply to questions about his or her former employer. For example, you might say something like "Well, we've decided not to dwell on the past. We're focusing on the future and its opportunities."

» 7. Remind your partner honestly of his or her skills, abilities and achievements. Be specific. Speak about his or her successes in detail.

» 8. Let your partner know repeatedly of your confidence in him or her and the fact that he or she overcame setbacks before and can do so again. Stress that this situation is only temporary.

Take heart from Elaine, who talked James back up from the depths of a severe depression and into a very successful new career. "It was like it was a challenge to me," she says. "He had to do it, but I had to help him. Often it was just a matter of talking to him and saying, 'Yes, I know you can,' and giving him books to read. I would go to the library, and I went to see the minister and asked if he could suggest some books. I was looking for books by people who'd been through similar situations. I'd read them, too, so we could discuss them. I was mainly showing him that other people had been down there, too. Like when Winston Churchill was fired years ago, he had a nervous breakdown and he built a brick wall all around his house. In other words, he wanted to close himself in, and I used to tell James, 'It's a natural thing. When people have been fired, they don't want to see people and they don't want anybody to see them, even Churchill.' I was showing him he wasn't alone in the world."

» 9. Help out with the job search in any way that is comfortable for both of you. This might mean scanning the paper for ads, suggesting people to contact, taking telephone messages and assisting with the resumé. Do what is reasonable and manageable, given your own commitments.

» 10. Discussing the job search can be a big help to the job seeker, but it might also be tricky, because your partner could be extremely sensitive to any suggestion that you are demanding an account of his or her time. Gabriella handles it this way: "I never, ever say, 'What have you done today?' because there could be days when he hasn't done very much. I say, 'Have you had a good day? Did anything interesting happen?' I'm not asking for an accounting. It's just casual conversation, and some days I know he'd rather not be asked at all, so I wait for him to open up when he feels like it."

» 11. We found that some couples think it helpful to set aside a particular time to discuss how the search has been going. Usually it's once a week, and part of their agreement is to not discuss the subject in between. This meets a spouse's need to know what's happening without appearing to be a nag, and it frees the job seeker from having to explain his or her activities every day.

» 12. In one respect, your partner is probably no different from anyone else. No one likes looking for work, at least not initially, so they dream up little excuses to avoid the search or not pursue it with the vigor of which they are capable. This may be because they need more time to get over the firing, or because of the various fears we mentioned previously. Once most people get going and receive some positive response to their efforts, they become quite involved in their searches. As the search extends, however, some job seekers find it difficult to sustain their motivation and can be very creative in coming up with good reasons not to call this contact or write those letters, and some will busy themselves with household projects and other activities. In short, the balance between the search and recreation will be out of whack.

» 13. If, early in the search, you feel your partner is avoiding getting on with it, be patient. If the search has been going on for some time, though, and you sense that the search is losing momentum, you might want to ask if he or she would like to talk about it. And, we should add, many job seekers' spouses have told us that nagging doesn't work. Understanding, support and gentle, optimistic encouragement are better bets, and sometimes saying nothing is the best course of action.

» 14. Finally, we'd like to address two persistent questions we heard from the people we interviewed. First of all, many of them wondered why their partners were not allowed to remain in their jobs until they had found new positions. The primary answer is that most people who've stayed on the job for any length of time after being given notice have found the situation increasingly uncomfortable, both for themselves and their colleagues. In other words, from the moment notice is given, that company and that job are history, so it is almost always best to make the physical break, as well as the psychological one, as quickly as possible and get on with the task of finding a new job.

The second question concerns some job seekers' temptation to tell prospective employers that they are still employed or that they resigned from their last job. These smoke screens are easily blown away by good interviewers and reference checkers. Also, the grapevine is often the most important source that employers tap into these days. Even if the person is hired, the truth is bound to come out and seriously undermine his or her credibility with the new employer.

In another wrinkle on this, one of our colleagues knows a man who did convince potential employers that he had resigned because his new responsibilities were not challenging enough. Even so, he was still not hired by anyone. Finally our colleague made some inquiries on his behalf and found that none of the interviewers who had talked to the man wanted anyone with his judgment working for them. After all, how could anyone with a modicum of common sense leave a good position without having something else lined up? As our colleague puts it, "People who say they've resigned from their last job risk being placed in one of three categories: dishonest, so well off they don't need to work, or just plain dumb."

Chapter Four

The Job Search

This chapter is different from those that have come before it and those that will follow, in that there are no coping suggestions at the end. The reason for this is that the entire chapter is a description of how one goes about finding a job in today's highly competitive marketplace and, as such, is in itself an extended series of coping notes. We'll be going into the various search procedures in some detail, but first we'd like to answer a few of the questions that, in our work as outplacement consultants, we hear most frequently from our clients' spouses. The first one has probably occurred to you already.

> *My partner is the one looking for a job, so why do you want to tell me what a job search entails?*

We have a number of reasons. As we noted back in the Limbo chapter, one of the most persistent frustrations that spouses face at this time is their sense of helplessness. They can't fix the situation. Only their partners can do that—by finding another job. Worse, like the majority of their job-seeking mates, most spouses have no idea of the time and effort that a well-conducted job search requires. Nor do they have any conception of the many search-related anxieties their partners may be wrestling with. Without this information many spouses become anxious about the job search process. This further increases their own stress and often leads to needless conflict or tension at home. In our work we hear about it all the time.

Therefore, this chapter is an effort to demystify the job search process. We hope it will help prepare you mentally for what lies ahead, thus easing some of your anxieties and preventing or defusing some of the tensions that might arise in your household. We strongly believe that when a couple share both the same goal and an understanding of what it takes to reach that goal, chances are the resulting teamwork will make the road smoother and perhaps even shorter.

Hold it. What's this teamwork bit? Just a second ago, you said only my partner can look for a job and I'm just a spectator.

That's true, in the sense that you cannot go out, pound the pavement and knock on doors on your partner's behalf. Nor can you go to job interviews with him or her. However, there are two extremely important home-front considerations where your partnership in the search is essential.

The first has to do with those search-related anxieties. At the root of these is the fact that it is not only spouses who don't know what a job search involves, their out-of-work partners may be completely ignorant of the process, too. In fact, this is almost certainly the case if they were hired straight out of school and have never worked for anyone other than their original employers; or if new jobs have always simply fallen into their laps through sheer chance or via recruitment agencies, headhunters and the like. In short, many people have never really had to look for a job in their lives.

Thus, after a layoff, people who may be extremely skilled in their own professions suddenly find themselves faced with a task that is crucial to their future, but which they do not know how to do well! This is one of the main reasons for the existence of outplacement consulting firms, which we will be discussing shortly. What we are talking about here is that first essential element of your partnership in the job search, which more than anything else is largely a matter of your being aware of the following:

» 1. Even though people get fired they still do have a job, and that job is finding another job.

» 2. At first they probably won't know how to do that job proficiently, which will cause them considerable anxiety.

» 3. This anxiety will be piled atop all the other anxieties, self-doubts, grief and frustrations that were dumped on them when they were fired. Even when they learn how to do an effective job search, there will still be many anxious moments for both them and their spouses.

Consequently, one of the best ways for spouses to help their job-seeking partners *and themselves* get through the job search period is to see that they do it together. On your part, one of the basics here is understanding, not only the rudimentary search techniques, but also the source and nature of the anxieties your partner will be contending with as he or she learns and applies those techniques.

> *Okay, what's the second element of the job search partnership?*

We're glad you asked, because this brings us to the point of the whole chapter. That is, your objective as a couple should not be just any old job.

Rather, your partner should be looking for what in our profession is called a "good fit." Your partner should be out searching for the job that best fits his or her skills, interests, personality, choice of work environment, preference in management style and many other factors, including, of course, the appropriate level of pay and benefits. In short, we are recommending with all our heart that your partner stick to the search until he or she finds the position that is most consistent with his or her goals as an individual and your goals as a couple. It would be very difficult to exaggerate the importance of this point.

> *Yes, but we're still talking about my partner's job. Where does the couple part come in?*

At the most basic level, if people enjoy their work, they will generally arrive home in the evening feeling happy and fulfilled, with obvious benefits to their family life. Also, if they are working at a place where the people and the corporate culture match their temperament, there is less chance of them being let go as a result of personality conflicts, which in turn will lessen the likelihood of their families having to live through another job search. In the previous chapter we pointed to Agnes, whose husband panicked and took a job he hates in a place he dislikes. As a result, both he and his family are miserable. His wife has little to look forward to other than a prolonged Limbo period she can't avoid, because it will continue regardless of whether he stays in that job or quits or is fired and has to begin the job search process all over again.

That, then, is a couple's basic stake in the quality of the new job. But we have also met couples who have taken this several steps farther, and viewed the firing as a marvelous opportunity to stop and think about their mutual goals and values. For example, in future chapters we will see how some former workaholics radically reassessed their values and made a point of taking jobs that gave them more time with their spouses and children.

> *But again, my partner's the one who chooses the job. From the spouse's point of view, what you are describing sounds like a pretty passive partnership.*

Not at all. Your input into the process is crucial, both to you as an individual and as your mate's partner.

To illustrate, let's consider a situation that arises very frequently. The nature of the job seeker's work means that he or she must at least think about applying for jobs in other cities. The best tack for spouses who find themselves in this situation is to face that fact and take steps to ensure that any move they make will meet as many of their own needs as possible. To that end, they might make a list of what a move must provide them in terms of their role as parents (good schools and such), in terms of their own careers and interests, and their overall view of their marriages. Doing this and then discussing the results with their partners will accomplish two things. It will help reduce their anxiety about a possible move, and above all, it will make their specific needs a large factor in their partners' decisions to apply for certain jobs and, ultimately, whether to accept them.

Which brings us to the point we wish to make here. Even when a possible move is not an issue, a spouse's input should still be an essential part of his or her partner's job search. For one thing, a spouse's insights into the partner's strengths and weaknesses, skills, and what types of jobs he or she might be good at is invaluable information. But more than anything, as we noted in reply to the last question, a termination is truly an opportunity for a couple to reassess their priorities and goals and, if need be, make significant adjustments to the way they have been living. Those workaholics we noted earlier returned to work determined to maintain a healthy balance between their careers and their family life. In doing so, they of course gained a lot for themselves. But their families were winners, too.

Ian, for example, told us how his wife's dismissal shocked her into re-evaluating what she wanted out of life. "It wouldn't be unkind to say Victoria had always been driven to succeed and terrified of failure," Ian said. "But when she was fired, she got a tremendous amount of encouragement from her family and friends and she realized how important these people are to her. Then one night, just as I was falling asleep, she suddenly said, 'Do you realize that in the ten years since I left college, my circle of family and friends has shrunk to about a third of what it was? Some don't call me any more, probably because I don't make the time to call them.' I had almost dozed off, but then she said, 'That means I've been totally selfish. I haven't even really considered you.' Well, that got my attention. I sat up and we talked for a long time. She said, 'I've only thought about what I'm doing and where I'm going. Whether you were there or not was almost irrelevant. But now I know how much I want you here and how much I want to spend time with my parents, because they're not going to be around forever.' I mean, that was the beginning of a big change in her, which isn't to say she's no longer ambitious. She now has a better sense of how to balance family, friends and work. Instead of wanting to be a vice president in five years, she's willing to do it in ten."

In the best of all possible job searches, both spouses will be genuine partners. In one heartening interview we conducted, the wife of a man who recently lost his job as a result of downsizing, consistently used the words "our job search." It seemed as if it was as much her search as her husband's. When both parties are committed to finding the right job fit, tensions at home are reduced, and each partner gains extra strength from the knowledge that they are working through this crisis together toward a common goal.

> *Earlier you mentioned outplacement consultants. Will they find my partner a job?*

No. Outplacement consultants help fired employees prepare themselves to conduct effective job searches, then coach them through the process. The key word here is help. We do not find work for people.

In most cases, outplacement consulting begins immediately after a firing. That is, consultants are frequently on site, ready to meet with fired employees immediately after their termination meetings. They are there to explain the service that is being provided and, if need be, act as a sounding board should the fired employees wish to vent their feelings about what has just happened. The consultants help them to organize their thoughts and caution them about some of the mistakes people tend to make at this time. For example, one common error is for fired employees to panic and start calling friends and contacts in the industry right away. All this does is alert the contacts to the callers' distress at a time when they are likely to come across as angry, disorganized, bitter and distraught—a sure-fire way to turn off these valuable sources of help.

Generally, the consultants and their clients meet again the very next day. The consultants outline their firms' services in greater detail and they get to work. At our firm we offer:

- Financial counseling
- Career planning and job target identification
- Assessment of clients' suitability for going into business for themselves, should they be interested in that direction
- Preparation of references
- Effective resumé and letter preparation
- Job search coaching, which encompasses the identification of job prospects and marketing one's skills and oneself via networking, direct mail, ad responses and recruiters
- Practice in effective telephone and face-to-face interviews
- Evaluation of job offers

- Compensation negotiations

- Administrative support in the form of office space and secretarial help.

Who pays for all this?

In the majority of cases the fired employee's former employer. The employee doesn't have to pay for anything. However, there are some organizations that can be hired directly by individuals if they haven't received this service from their former employers.

Why would the company provide this service for someone they decided not to keep in their employ?

While the company no longer has a place for someone, it is still interested in the former employee finding work that suits his or her interests and abilities as soon as possible. Part of this is plain good will. Part is good old-fashioned self-interest. Providing job search assistance soothes the corporate conscience; and when re-employment consulting is combined with fair severance payments, it reduces the likelihood of having to face unnecessary lawsuits.

In other words, even though this consulting firm is directly helping my partner, it's working for the former employer, as well.

True, it may appear that the consultant has two masters—the company that sponsors the service and the recipient of the service. And the consulting firm certainly does wish to remain on good terms with the company. However, the primary focus of an outplacement consultant's work is on helping the fired employee find a new job that is a good fit for his or her capabilities and needs.

> ## *Does this consulting service extend to spouses?*

While it is not yet widespread in our industry, we are beginning to see examples of more extensive services being offered to spouses. In fact, our research and this book are the result of a growing awareness by our profession of the great need for comprehensive spousal services, which we hope will be recognized and met by employers and consulting firms in the near future. For now, we can only hope that you will find our book the next best thing to personal consultation and a valuable guide throughout your partner's job search.

> ## *And how long will the search last?*

We are really reluctant to suggest a figure that will apply to your situation, because each person's search is different. In our experience, the average is four to six months. In recessionary times, the average can be eight or nine months. The length of a job search is generally determined by how diligently people work at their searches, their particular circumstances and a little bit of luck. It is also affected by the health of the job market in their community, the job turnover in the industry in which they are seeking work and the level at which they hope to find a position. For example, in some engineering fields there may be a high turnover of middle-level managers and finding such positions close to home is relatively easy. On the other hand, if your partner was a vice president of research and development in a small, highly specialized corner of the aerospace industry and wants to find a similar job, chances are such openings are rare, and you will have to plan accordingly. Some senior executives we know have actually planned for twelve- and even eighteen-month job searches.

There are many other factors that can affect the length of a job search, but the main point here is to not expect immediate success. As we cautioned earlier, picking a number like three months out of the air and making that a deadline will only add to your anxiety. A better tactic is to allow as much time as possible and prepare a budget to see you through this period. That way you'll have the security of knowing you can manage while you and your partner hold out for the right job. If it comes along sooner than you expected, so much the better. You'll have money in the bank to pay for a well-needed vacation or to help pay off the mortgage.

> *How are we going to have any money left in the bank? My partner's been off work for two weeks now and doesn't seem to have done a thing. What's going on?*

There could be several answers here. For one thing, fired people are often simply exhausted and in need of time to recover from the months of stress that preceded their dismissal. Also, the firing itself was probably devastating. And as we noted earlier in this chapter, many people do not know how to go about looking for a job. As a result, they may be feeling shy, embarrassed, confused and even afraid.

Ideally, the starting point is three or four weeks of intense preparation before people even begin to reply to ads and do all the other things you expect to see your partner doing.

The Search

When we say your partner's job is to find another job, we are not plucking a convenient figure of speech out of the air. A job search is a full-time occupation. To be more specific, job seekers are conducting major marketing campaigns. They are trying to find companies that are looking for people like them, and to achieve this goal, it is essential that they divide their energy and resources between the two major job markets: the visible market and the hidden one.

The visible market includes all job openings that become public knowledge via newspaper advertisements, executive recruiters and placement agencies. The hidden market encompasses jobs that have not yet been (and may never be) made public. Accordingly, only a few people know about them, and in some cases they are still hardly more than ideas in the minds of managers who are waiting for the right person to come along and make them a reality. Because so few people know about these jobs, the competition for them is much less and often nonexistent. In our experience, more than two-thirds of all job seekers find their new jobs in the hidden market, and we strongly advise our clients to devote the majority of their time to uncovering these concealed opportunities.

To do that, and to tap the visible market, as well, is where the marketing campaign we mentioned comes in. In all, it is a five-phase operation:

» 1. ADJUSTING This involves the various things your partner and you need to do before the job search actually begins. These include:

- Initial crisis management
- Arranging the family finances

- Setting up an office at home
- Time management

» 2. PLANNING   Everything your partner has to do before he or she approaches the job market. The tasks here encompass:

- Career assessment
- Determining job targets
- Revising or preparing the resumé
- Putting references in place
- Market research
- Developing his or her initial contacts list

» 3. DOING   Finally, after three or four weeks of preparation, your partner will at last be ready to tackle the job market. He or she does this by:

- Networking. Putting his or her contacts list to work. This is by far the most important part of the search, and we'll have a lot to say about it later.
- Sending marketing letters
- Replying to ads
- Contacting search firms
- Preparing for and attending interviews
- Getting feedback from interviews

» 4. EVALUATING   There are two activities here. They are:

- Continually reviewing how he or she's doing in the job search and looking for improvements

- Assessing job opportunities in relation to the goals he or she has (with you) established

» 5. NEGOTIATING AND DECIDING If a job offer does appear to be consistent with these goals, your partner will then have to negotiate the terms, including the compensation package, with the prospective employer. If suitable terms are reached, you and your partner will then have to decide whether he or she should accept the offer.

The tasks included in the planning and doing phases are aspects of a two-part strategy, which is the heart of an effective job search: (*a*) using every available method to reach potential employers and (*b*) generating a high volume of face-to-face contacts with people in the job market your partner is exploring.

Phase One: Adjusting

Initial Crisis Management

The purpose of this section is to come to terms with a number of issues and sort out various administrative details that will get in the way of a well-prepared, clearheaded job search. The tasks include:

- Giving yourselves a day or so to catch your breath, tell the children and others about the firing and work out a common explanation for it

- Evaluating the severance package, which is a key step in making a quick, clean break with the former employer. The main question is, "Is the package a fair one?" You may wish to consult a lawyer on this. If you do, select one who (*a*) specializes in employment law and (*b*) will let you, as a couple, keep control of the situation while making informed decisions. We have found that until the severance package has been agreed on, most people continue to be tied to their former companies and find it extremely difficult to focus on their job search. Therefore it is very important to consider carefully any decision to begin legal proceedings, which could tie up your time, financial resources and energy for many months, even two or three years

- Sorting out your finances, which will mean determining how much money you have and figuring out how to make the best use of it over an extended job search

- Registering at the local unemployment office, when appropriate

- Arranging for continuation of essential medical and life insurance coverage

- Such administrive details as retrieving your partner's personal effects from the office, rearranging or adjusting social and business commitments, buying or returning the company car, perhaps acquiring a new car and transferring accounts to a bank closer to home.

Setting Up the In-Home Office

The establishment of such an office can be fraught with disruption and strife. Even if your partner's re-employment consultant has provided office space, it is likely that he or she will still need a comfortable spot to work from at home, preferably an entire room, though even a portion of one will do, as long as the space is clearly designated for the job search and nothing else. If the search is at all thorough, you'll probably be astonished by the huge piles of newspapers and documents that will accumulate and the amount of letter writing and resumé drafting that is required.

Some spouses are happy to do their partners' typing, feeling that it's their contribution to the search. On the other hand, some job seekers hire typists, to give their resumés and correspondence an extra professional touch, while still others rent or buy computers and prepare their own documents.

One place where the entire family can help is in taking phone messages. Even if you have an answering machine (and you should), you'll all be taking messages now and then, so don't wait for the kids to forget or garble an important call before you act. Make sure that they know they are supposed to write every message down and that they are to repeat the spellings of names and companies and confirm the numbers and addresses they have been given.

One woman we interviewed found herself in an awkward situation because one of her husband's contacts kept returning his calls while he was out. The fellow kept asking what her husband wanted. "Is he looking for work?" the man would say. Knowing that a "yes" answer to this question can turn some contacts off, the woman always said her husband had some ideas to discuss with the man, which was true, but it didn't make her feel any more comfortable. The best policy when you are asked such direct questions is to plead ignorance of the details of your mate's business and promise that he or she will get in touch soon.

Time Management

As your partner prepares for and then embarks upon the job search, he or she will do best to create and stick to a weekly work schedule, resisting the all but inevitable pressures to indulge in hobbies, to increase commitments to community work and to do all the household chores you can probably imagine. We're not saying your partner shouldn't have a bit of fun or help around the house, but you should remember that the search is a full-time job and resist the urge to say things like "Since you're not working, maybe this is a good time to redo the basement." Also, when people do make their search a full-time job, their spouses find it enormously reassuring. In the Limbo chapter we noted how dismayed Linda was when her husband bought a nice warm track suit and seemed to be getting ready to spend the winter hibernating in his basement office. Conversely, Pat told us how pleased she was to see her husband up, dressed in a suit and on his way out the door to continue his search almost every day. He maintained a productive balance between face-to-face meetings and at-home office work, and his action-oriented, positive attitude plainly told her that the Limbo period was indeed going to end someday. This did a lot to relieve her of any fears she may have had that he would become a couch potato and that she would end up as the family's sole breadwinner.

Dressing the Part

If your partner puts aside his or her business attire and starts wearing clothing more appropriate for weekends, he or she will be unable to respond immediately to a request for an interview.

Moreover, the way people dress affects their morale and their self-respect, which is very important when they are unemployed, because they have a big job keeping themselves up all the time. Thus their way of dressing is a visible sign to their spouses, themselves and others that they are taking their situation seriously. To cite only one example, should they run into friends on the street during business hours, casual clothing will call undue attention to their lack of a job and perhaps raise doubts about their interest in finding a new one. They will, in short, have forgotten that dressing the part is important not only for their morale, but also their professional image.

Leslie was aware of the importance of always dressing in a businesslike manner from observing a relative who'd been out of work. Thus, when she saw Paul dressed as if for golf and about to go down to our office one morning shortly after his dismissal, she knew what to do: "I said to him, 'Don't you dare leave this house any day without a suit and a tie,' and he never did. I don't mean we have the sort of relationship where I can tell him to go back upstairs and change. We have a good talking relationship, and he did it because we talked about it. He saw I felt very strongly about this, and soon he did, too." At such times, a good appearance is not a luxury, it's a necessity.

Phase Two: Planning

Career Assessment

At our firm, one of the fundamental tasks with all new clients is to determine what sort of jobs will be a good fit in terms of their skills, interests, experience and life circumstances. To that end, one of the very first things we do is ask them to prepare an inventory of their skills and achievements, which has enormous practical and therapeutic value.

Basically, the inventory is a list of their prior work experience, but we don't stop there. When the initial list is done, we ask them to look back at each of their jobs over the past ten to fifteen years and think about the aspects of those jobs that they enjoyed and did well. These are their core achievements. Then they are asked to list hobbies and any volunteer work they have enjoyed, for these are achievements, as well, and they are encouraged to think about them in terms of the knowledge and skills they applied in doing them.

With some thought, most clients are able to compile an impressive record of accomplishment, both at and away from work. However, studying each experience in order to determine the specific skills and knowledge they've developed is a much more difficult task. If your partner needs help with this, there is an excellent checklist in the appendix to Richard Bolles' *What Color Is Your Parachute?* The author calls it "The Quick Job-Hunting Map." Essentially it's a detailed list of skills, and for each achievement he has noted, readers are asked to scan the list and pick out the skills they applied to, or learned from, the experience.

The purpose of all this work is to help restore the clients' confidence, clarify their career directions and goals and add concrete detail to their written and in-person marketing efforts. In terms of direction and goals, this exercise will help them determine whether they want to continue in their previous line of work or opt for a major career change. It will also help them define and rank their job targets in terms of the nature of the work, type of industry, preferred level in the organization, compensation range, upward mobility, vacation time, key peers and subordinates, characteristics of the boss, geographical location and all the other factors that we call "job fit criteria." In short, even before they begin their job searches, a comprehensive skills inventory will enable them to know, in detail, exactly what they are, or should be, looking for.

As well as the information one compiles oneself, your partner might also obtain suggestions on the best job fit and useful views of his or her strengths and soft spots from you, a good friend, a career counselor or industrial psychologist and former colleagues from the previous five years. Talking with people who've seen him or her in action will provide a particularly vivid view of your partner's attributes, which can be tested against a number of self-perceptions.

Remember, the clearer people are in their own minds about who they are and what they are looking for, the better they can focus their efforts on the jobs and companies that suit them best. Moreover, this information has uses beyond the selection of their job targets and job fit criteria. That is, it is also the raw material for their resumés and marketing letters, and it is indispensable when they describe their job needs to interviewers and contacts.

Revising or Preparing the Resumé

Prospective employers can receive hundreds of resumés in response to an ad. The decision makers do not see even a fraction of them. The submissions are first screened by other people. A few are forwarded for closer consideration, and from this handful, a tiny number of applicants are invited for interviews. The question then is, how did those few resumés make it through the screening process? The quick answer is that something about them grabbed those first readers. Undoubtedly the authors of the winning resumés demonstrated that they had the range of skills needed for the job in question. Moreover, they probably also demonstrated by the tone of their resumés and the presentation of themselves and their work experience, that they have a talent for clear thought and organization; that they care about quality in everything they do; and that they have a genuine interest in applying their talents to the challenges offered by that particular job.

But it's not good enough to present just a simple list of details, no matter how gripping each might be in itself. The whole document must be well organized and interesting to read, and this is where the writing becomes difficult.

However, there is a lot of help available. Advice on effective resumé and marketing letter writing is usually offered by outplacement consultants. Public libraries have many books on these subjects, and night schools and other adult education programs often offer courses in them.

Putting References in Place

Any genuinely interested employer will want to talk to two or three references before making a job offer, and it's best to compile them before the search begins. They should be people who can speak knowledgeably about your partner's past work experience, strengths and character. Permission to use them as references should be obtained beforehand, and if it seems likely that a prospective employer will call the references, your partner should phone them first, telling them to expect a call and describing the job and why it would be a good fit.

A frequent concern is the matter of what the former employer will say. A prospective employer will find it odd if the references don't include someone from your partner's last workplace, but people who have had difficulties with their former bosses are reluctant to cite them as references. Often this matter is taken care of at the termination meeting, with the person who is doing the firing explaining what the company will say if it is asked for a reference. If the issue has not been resolved and if the terminated employee has an outplacement consultant, the two of them can usually work out an agreement with the company on what will be said.

In any case, the former boss's name should be given as a reference. If your partner feels that this person's remarks might get in the way of job offers, it will probably be best if your partner just tells prospective employers that the previous working relationship was difficult at times. Then, with the understanding that the prospective employer will still want to talk to his or her former boss, your partner can ask that this person's remarks be considered in light of what the other references have to say.

Market Research. Or, What Are They Doing in the Library?

Good job searches are built on good research, and almost all the information your partner needs is in the industrial directories, trade journals, business magazines and newspapers to be found at any sizable public library. The object of this research is fivefold:

- Identifying target industries and jobs

- Identifying the companies where those jobs can be found

- Identifying the executives in those companies who have the authority to hire someone like your partner

- Getting a firm grasp of trends and developments in target industries, sectors and companies

- Identifying possible contacts.

Preparing the Initial Contacts List

This is the first step in the networking process and should not be ignored, for one's personal contacts are the main door to the hidden job market.

By this we do not mean that most people who find new jobs get them from people they already know. Rather, they create a situation in which their initial contacts (people they do know) direct them to other contacts . . . and so on, until finally, after following up all of these leads, they find themselves face-to-face with the people who have the right job openings and the authority to hire them.

The starting point is those initial contacts, and they are virtually everyone that you and your partner know, including the names that emerged from the library research. When this list is complete, your partner will be ready to begin looking for a job.

Phase Three: Doing

Networking

Networking is the method by which job seekers put their contact lists to work and gain access to the hidden job market.

The ultimate goal is to end up sitting across the desk from people who have the right job opportunities and the authority to hire the right person. However, unless your partner is very lucky, this won't happen for quite a while. Thus, for all job seekers, the fundamental activity in networking is calling people who might bring them closer to that ultimate goal and arranging face-to-face meetings with them. The starting point is their initial contact list. Putting it to work is simply a matter of calling contacts and suggesting a brief meeting. The purpose of these meetings is to let them know they are in the market, to discuss the market with them, solicit their ideas, suggestions and advice, enquire about possible target firms, and, above all, get at least two more names to add to their contact lists! And that is how a contact network grows.

As their networks begin to grow, job seekers soon find themselves calling people they don't know. However, they will know the people who gave them their names. Thus they can begin each call by introducing themselves and saying that "So and So" over at "Such and Such" suggested they get in touch. The key here is to make it clear that they have not called to ask about a specific job. Rather, they are calling to ask for a few minutes of the person's time to discuss the general job market in the field of work in which they are interested. Also, they should not let the call become a telephone interview. Their primary goal is to make an appointment and get off the line.

However, in a very competitive job market, the person may want some more information before agreeing to see your partner. Before they can be helpful, they may need to know your mate's job targets, and this is where the hours of preparation pay off. When your partner is able to identify clearly and concisely what he or she is looking for, contacts will probably be more receptive. In our experience, people are more willing to help job seekers who have done their homework and are more focussed in their goals.

At first your partner may find calling strangers and trying to arrange meetings with them a very frightening experience. But after the first six or seven calls, it will become easier. He or she may even come to see it as the absorbing challenge it is. But no matter how enjoyable it becomes, your partner should be prepared for some people to respond with a flat "no." Others, while not actually saying no to a meeting, will be reluctant, hesitant and even uncooperative. Most contacts, though, will try to be helpful. Sometimes surprisingly so.

The end result will be more meetings, more names, more calls and more and more meetings. After dozens of such meetings, you might begin to wonder if the whole exercise is getting absurd. It isn't. At each meeting your partner is gathering both specific and general market intelligence; practicing his or her communications skills; and increasing the odds of eventually finding the ultimate contact—the one who just happens to have the right job opening.

As your partner goes about learning how to make it work for him or her, the two of you might consider the following tips:

- In approaching his or her initial contacts, your partner may feel especially shy about putting the arm on friends and appearing to be begging for a job. Also, many spouses told us that their partners feel their skills should speak for themselves and that networking is somehow beneath them. The answer to such objections is that your partner is indeed skilled; in fact, somewhere out in that vast marketplace there are people who really need those skills. The only thing is, your partner has to find them. This is best done by marketing his or her skills, and the most productive way of doing so is by creating a contact network. Telling friends and acquaintances that he or she is in the market, and seeking their aid and advice, is not begging—it's advertising.

- It will be a great help if your partner really can think of him- or herself as a marketer of a valuable set of skills, rather than as a supplicant. This not only helps job seekers reduce whatever shyness they might feel, it also helps them deal with the rejection they will encounter at all stages of the job search. There is no way of avoiding it: hundreds of people will be saying no to your partner in one way or another, and both of you must somehow come to realize that this type of rejection is not a personal afront.

- It's always a good idea for job seekers periodically to call their contacts again to let them know how the leads they were given worked out and ask if the contacts have thought of any further leads.

- It is important for job seekers to keep track of who they have called and what they talked about so they can refresh their memories about previous discussions before they call again.

- Your partner's networking time will be most efficiently used if he or she can set aside days for phoning and days for meetings.

- Many spouses asked us about the advisability of their partners taking consulting or contract assignments during the job search. Our answer is that there are several advantages. It can be a big morale booster and give them the confidence to turn down a wrong job. It also provides extra cash. And the contacts made through consulting and contracting can lead to a full-time job. The major disadvantage is similar to that faced by people who remain at their workplaces after they've been told they are going to be dismissed. They think it is easier to look for a job from a job, but their work for the company inevitably interferes with their job search. Similarly, consulting or contracting will divert time and energy from your partner's search.

- Finally, we must deal with an extremely effective but generally ignored aspect of networking: approaching people who cannot be reached via contacts. For example, during the research phase, job seekers will learn the names of managers in likely companies to whom they should really talk. But in the course of their networking they won't find anyone who knows these people. Therefore they won't be able to call them up and say " 'So and So' over at 'Such and Such' suggested I give you a call."

Most people are terrified at the very idea of approaching complete and utter strangers without such a hook. Yet this is an enormously effective job search method in that (*a*) it is an excellent way to reach people who would otherwise remain outside one's contact network; and (*b*) because other job seekers tend to avoid using this method, the competition is reduced. Generally the decision maker will not have an immediate opening and may not want to see someone only for an exploratory discussion. Your partner's task, then, is to arouse the target person's interest and, almost as if it were an inevitable result of the conversation, arrange a meeting date.

Your partner must be confident, positive and persistent; fully rehearsed in the message he or she wants to convey; and thick-skinned in the face of hostility or indifference. Your partner should also, we must add, be prepared for rejection. On average, it takes twelve calls to make direct contact with a target person, and contact is no guarantee of success. If only five percent of your partner's calls result in face-to-face meetings, he or she will be doing extremely well; and, of course, your partner can still ask the people who don't agree to a meeting for more names and send his or her resumé and a good covering letter to them. You never know when some little extra effort like that will pay off.

Marketing Letters

Another way of uncovering unadvertised positions in the hidden job market is to send brief letters to prospective employers. Each one should contain only enough information about the job seeker's strengths and interest in the company to excite the recipient's interest.

As in the drafting of a compelling resumé, creating a positive, enticing letter is a considerable challenge, but meeting it can be very worthwhile. At the same time, unless job seekers and their spouses understand the basic strategy of a direct mail campaign, it could become a source of recurring pain. A large number of spouses told us that one of the worst aspects of the job search was the daily arrival of negative replies to their partners' marketing letters. In time each one came to be seen as a personal slight, an inconsiderate and often heartless dismissal of a talented person's abilities.

It's true, a lot of replies are exactly that, but a lot of the pain suffered by these job seekers and their spouses arose simply because they didn't expect to get so many rejections. They were not aware that a very high rate of rejection is the norm and has absolutely nothing to do with their partners' abilities. Think of all the unsolicited mail that comes to your home. How often have you tossed it out with hardly a glance? You've probably even wondered why they bother wasting their time sending stuff to you. The answer is that the professionals who run direct mail campaigns start out with the realization that for every hundred items they mail, ninety-seven or ninety-eight recipients are going to be just like you and throw the material away. But they don't care about you. Their focus is on the two or three people who are going to buy their product.

So too for job seekers' direct mail campaigns. Most of the organizations they send their letters to will not have openings at that time, but some of them will. If they get two or three positive replies for every hundred letters, they will be doing very well, and they can substantially increase their success rate by following up each letter with a telephone call about ten days later.

Replying to Ads

There are a few basic points to remember. Both individual companies and search firms acting on behalf of companies place job ads in newspapers and trade journals. Although papers tend to run special careers sections a couple of times a week, jobs are advertised in the paper every day. Ads are often placed only once. Therefore it's advisable to check all local and national papers daily; and should your partner's job search extend to other cities, it's important to check their local papers on a daily basis, as well.

One tactic that few people know about is to look at back issues of newspapers for ads that were placed two to four weeks before the beginning of the job search. The reason for doing this is that it usually takes two to four months to fill a position, so these jobs are probably still open.

When answering an ad, it is important that your partner's reply details exactly how his or her background fits with the requirements outlined in the ad.

Contacting Search Firms

Search firms are known by several names: headhunters, executive recruiters and employment or placement agencies.

They try to find people to fill positions they know are available within certain organizations. For some openings, they place ads in newspapers and trade journals. They also look for people using their own contact networks and the resumés they have on file. The end result of their efforts is the presentation of a number of candidates to the organization concerned, which then interviews the candidates and decides which one to hire.

Search firms are well worth getting to know and are usually approached the same way as other contacts are solicited. That is, through one's contact network and by letters, phone calls and resumé submissions. The thing to remember about these firms is that while they can be a great help, they handle only a limited portion of all the jobs that are going at any given time and they are no substitute for a thorough search by the individual job seeker.

Interviews

Basically, interviews are opportunities for companies and prospective employees to size each other up, and the job seekers' goal is to obtain job offers, even if their initial impression is that they don't want to work for the firms in question.

The key to managing any interview well is preparation, which is mainly a matter of additional research and anticipating and rehearsing questions about one's skills, background, goals and knowledge of the company. You might be able to help your partner rehearse. He or she can also use a tape recorder; and, if he or she has one, the outplacement consultant will review the interview procedure, from what to wear to what questions to ask and how to answer interviewers' questions.

The really hard part, for both you and your partner, will come *after* the interview. So many spouses told us that the cruelest segment of the job search was while they were waiting for the telephone to ring and prospective employers to say "yes" or "no." More often than not, even when interviewers had promised to phone by a certain date, they did not, and some never called at all.

Frances described the effect such delays can have on a couple: "If someone says he's going to call the next morning and doesn't call until the next afternoon, it does terrible things to your mind. All you can think about is disaster. That happened to us a lot, and one time, someone said to Nick, 'I'll be in touch with you in two weeks,' and those two weeks were interminable. All you can do is wait. We went to a lot of shows in the evening. On weekends, we went skiing or up to his mother's—anything to get our minds off the wait."

The waiting is especially unbearable after a job seeker has been called back for additional interviews and the promise is brighter than ever. "We really thought he had it," Angela says. "But then, on the Friday, they said they had given the job to someone with more specialized experience. Percy called to tell me at work because he knew I was dying to know one way or the other. I could tell he felt as low as I did. Each time we put a lot of hope into something, we feel so high. We think, finally we're reaching the end, and then when we get another "no" and find ourselves back at square one, we're utterly wretched."

It's all but impossible for almost any couple to avoid such an emotional roller-coaster ride, but you can lessen its effects by being prepared for it; by not allowing yourselves to get too high or too low, no matter how promising a job may seem; by doing pleasant things to take your mind off the wait, the way Frances and Nick did; and, above all, by trying not to pin all your hopes on one particular job.

This last is accomplished by continuing to network, send marketing letters and reply to ads, even if your partner has had what seems to have been an excellent interview. In our experience, it is not uncommon for job seekers to slacken their search when they have a promising prospect, but many seemingly glittering opportunities will fall through before the search is over, and it's difficult and time-consuming to rekindle a search once it has slowed down. Also, there is no telling how long it will take an employer to reach a decision, or what the other candidates are offering. If the decision goes against you, as many will before the job search is over, the hurt and disappointment will be somewhat mitigated if your partner has a lot of other irons in the fire and the momentum of his or her search hasn't slackened.

Getting Feedback from Interviews

One reason interviewers don't get back to job applicants with a yes or no answer right away is that they are busy with other responsibilities. Sometimes they want to make sure their first choice has accepted the job, before rejecting the others. And some just can't bring themselves to deliver the bad news.

Whatever the reason, the spouses we talked to were almost universally critical of the cruel, seemingly needless delays they and their partners had to endure. One way to minimize the waiting is for your partner to periodically call the interviewer and ask where he or she stands. If your partner is finally told that he or she is no longer a candidate, it would be useful to know why. This kind of feedback is rarely offered, but some managers are willing to discuss the interview if the candidate asks. The result could be valuable advice on how your partner should improve his or her interview skills.

No part of the job search is easy, and sometimes it will seem as if you are going to be stuck on that emotional roller coaster forever. Rest assured, you won't be. Someday the ride will end, perhaps when you are least expecting it.

Here is how Frances and Nick's ride ended: "The chief interviewer was a man named Sam, and he said to Nick, 'I'll call you on Monday morning and let you know. That's when I'm making my decision.' Well, the following Monday, no phone call came, and we were both almost basket cases. By 4:00 p.m., I had to go out for a walk because I couldn't stand it any more. And by Monday night, we had it all figured out—he's not going to get the job. We were both really down. Then the next morning, Tuesday, I went off to the fitness center because I was still feeling bad. It's terrible. Every time it happens, you feel you have to start and build yourself up again and get motivated and put this one behind you and start over. When I came home, Nick was on the phone, but I didn't think anything of it. I just went upstairs to take a shower, and Nick came up behind me. I didn't know he was there till he said Sam had been on the phone, and he'd offered him the job. Well, it was so unexpected that all we could do was just hug each other and laugh ourselves silly. We couldn't believe it. We were on cloud nine with relief!"

Phase Four: Evaluating

Evaluating Progress

This is not so much a phase as a continuing activity. Throughout the job search, it is necessary for job seekers continually to assess their effectiveness and ensure that their focus is correct.

To that end, the responses to their marketing letters and the feedback they are getting from their contacts and the interviews they attend are all useful pieces of information. They help job seekers answer such questions as "Am I really targeting the right jobs and the right industries? Am I doing the right things to achieve my goals? Are there other things I might do, as well?"

A spouse's perceptions and concerns can be a very important contribution to the review process, so it might also be a good idea for you and your partner to set aside some time, say about every three months, to evaluate the search together. An important item on the agenda should be how it's going for you and the kids.

Evaluating Job Offers

When a job offer is finally made, there is great jubilation and relief. And worry: how can you tell if it's the right one? Maybe your partner will accept the job for the wrong reasons. The search has been going on for months now, your partner has been working extremely hard, his or her networking is beginning to pay off, so who's to say an even better job won't come along next week?

Such concerns are natural after investing so much time and torment in the job search, and the decision is one of the biggest a couple ever has to face. A big help here is the list of job fit criteria your partner drew up at the beginning of the search. Measuring offers against the criteria and taking current circumstances into account will make the couple's decision to accept or not somewhat easier. However, it is our experience that spouses generally back off at this moment, acknowledging that their partners are the ones who have to be happy in their work and only they can be the ultimate judges of a job's rightness.

The most common reasons for someone to jump into the wrong job are financial concerns, pride, pressure from family and other sources, and impatience with the job search. If these factors prevail, an air of panic can take over and objective evaluation of an offer becomes all but impossible.

A couple may rationalize the acceptance of a bad job by saying he or she can still look for a job from the new job. But, as we've noted, that rarely works. The job at hand takes precedence, leaving little time for the chores a proper job search demands. Also, people who employ this tactic run the risk of being perceived as job hoppers, thus damaging their credibility with prospective employers.

We can offer no blanket advice here. For instance, a couple of years ago, one of our clients was offered a wrong job. The offer came after a particularly long and hard search. The man's wife had been absolutely heroic in keeping the family going, frequently borrowing from relatives to help meet their monthly expenses. Yet when her husband told her about the offer, her immediate response was that he should say no. The job was not right for him or for them. She knew that he and she would only be miserable if he got trapped that way, so she was prepared to go on living hand to mouth until a job that was better came along.

As it happened, a right job came along quite quickly. Although we admire that woman tremendously and wholeheartedly agree with what she did, it is not our place to say that you should do the same if you are faced with a similar dilemma. Every couple has their own priorities, inner strengths and limits of endurance. Only they can make such decisions. All we can do is point out the factors that should be taken into consideration.

Phase Five: Negotiating and Deciding

A decision to accept a job does not necessarily mean your partner has to accept the company's first offer. Before making the final decision and actually saying yes, your partner can negotiate the terms of employment, including the compensation package.

A frequent stumbling block here is that after people have been out of work for some time, they and their spouses may be hesitant about trying to negotiate a better deal. Usually this is out of fear that the offer will be withdrawn if they get picky. However, if your partner approaches negotiation flexibly and avoids putting him- or herself and the prospective employer in a take-it-or-leave-it situation, the company will most likely be willing to listen.

Essential to successful negotiation on your mate's part is a clear grasp of the bottom line—the basic package that he or she wishes to obtain. Of course, throughout the negotiations, it may be necessary to suggest or consider concessions that your partner or the company might make. Thus the ultimate goal, no matter how the negotiations turn out, is that both your partner and the employer emerge with their dignity intact and no damage to their future working relationship.

The ideal position is to have more than one offer to consider at the same time. In reality, though, it is unusual to receive two offers simultaneously. But if your partner receives one offer and another seems to be in the offing, he or she may try to negotiate some extra time to consider the first offer in the hope that the second one will come in, as well.

A variation of this is the case where a job seeker will get an offer from one company but be more excited by another opportunity that is still in the development stage. In this situation, your partner will have to negotiate the offer he or she already has and then come to a decision about whether to accept it or decline it and hope an offer is made by the other organization. If your partner declines a job for this reason, it is important that you are both comfortable with the simple fact that there is absolutely no guarantee that the second offer will materialize.

As you can see, planning and conducting an effective, comprehensive job search is a considerable undertaking, requiring a lot of hard work, persistence and continual motivation on the parts of both spouses. We have continually found that when a couple approaches the search as partners, committed to goals they set at the beginning and prepared for the tasks they will meet along the way, the journey is easier and smoother for both. The bonus is that this partnership also enriches their relationship.

That relationship is the subject of our next chapter.

Chapter Five

The Two of You

For better or worse, a firing brings a marriage sharply into focus, throwing a bright, unwavering light on everything there is to be seen, whether it's a relationship's inherent flaws in communication or a couple's fundamental strengths and unshakable love. Each partner reacts to the event and its aftershocks as an individual and is also affected by (and affects) the other's reactions. Thus both partners put themselves and the assumptions that underlie their relationship to one of the most severe tests a couple can face.

Nearly all the spouses we spoke with reported some difficult moments in their relationships after their partners' dismissals and throughout the subsequent job searches. Most were able to ride out these storms and learn valuable lessons. Many couples became closer and their marriages were strengthened.

Others, unfortunately, became stuck in their problems. Why? How is it that some relationships can withstand and even be improved by the crisis, while others seem to be shattered irreparably?

For us, one of the most useful tools in studying and understanding the often wildly diverse situations we encountered is the contract theory of marriage, which is both suitably comprehensive and pleasingly simple. As outlined by Bernice Hunt and Clifford J. Sager in their conclusive book, *Intimate Partners: Hidden Patterns in Love Relationships,* the contract theory states that each partner enters marriage with a set of expectations of what he or she will give to the other and receive in return. Hunt and Sager call such expectations "covenants." And these, they say, deal with every aspect of a couple's life: relationships with friends, achievements, sex, power, leisure time, money, closeness, children, and so forth. The way any couple gets along together is a direct reflection of how well they live up to the terms of each other's covenants.

This applies, Hunt and Sager add, even if a couple is not consciously aware of the covenants with which they entered their relationship. Some couples have congruent covenants.

That is, consciously or unconsciously, each partner expects to give and get similar things. Other couples enjoy complementary covenants, which means that although each partner's set of expectations is different, they combine well and make for a satisfying relationship. In both congruent and complementary situations, the partners consciously or unconsciously meld their individual covenants into a mutual agreement, or contract, by which each understands what he or she will give to and get from the relationship. Still other couples have conflicting covenants—clashing expectations, which create endless trouble for the partners, with each side tending to be disappointed in or resentful of the other.

Whether a couple has congruent, complementary or conflicting expectations, a firing is a direct assault on their marital contract. Simultaneously, each party experiences a personal crisis, which, although caused by the same event, is substantially different from the other's. For both parties, new needs and expectations arise. New patterns of behavior emerge. The give-get balance of the relationship may be tested to its limit and prove to be inappropriate or insufficient. As one woman described it, "all the rules get thrown up in the air," and if the contract is not flexible enough to accommodate these new requirements, or the couple is unable or unwilling to renegotiate their agreement, the resulting disappointments and strife can destroy their marriage.

At the end of this chapter we will take a close look at the overall ways in which, with varying success, different couples met this sudden need to review the terms of their marital contracts. First, however, we'd like to turn the spotlight on certain individual aspects, or focal points, of the marital relationship and give you a more detailed look at how some of the many components of a contemporary marriage are affected by a dismissal crisis. Although most of the spouses we interviewed instinctively knew what was going on, not one spoke to us specifically in terms of contract negotiations or clause-by-clause revisions of their agreements. More than anyone, they knew that even at the best of times marriage bears no resemblance to a sedate, well-ordered meeting of lawyers. Marriage is real life, and as such, rarely unfolds in the neat, logical, convenient manner we would like it to. This is especially true after a firing. As a result, even though these spouses and their mates were amending their marital contracts, they were performing not like lawyers, but actors who have been summoned without warning to improvise roles on a strange stage.

The Focal Points

The following are the areas our interviews revealed as the most likely to undergo change in the aftermath of a dismissal. Each holds the potential for conflict and dissatisfaction if the changes challenge either partner's needs and expectations. At the same time, a flexible response to such challenges can lead a couple to greater closeness and intimacy.

Daily Routines

In previous chapters we noted how some spouses were greatly disturbed by their partners' sudden and generally thoughtless presence at home during the day. We also noted that many other spouses were delighted to have their mates around more. One of these was Emily, a homemaker. When we met her, Wayne, her husband, was in the eighteenth month of his job search. When we asked if his time at home had brought them closer, she said "no." They already had a strong relationship and were using this unexpected time together to pursue their common interests. They also made a point of spending some time apart; and for one brief period, Wayne had worked full-time as the unpaid chairman of an important city parks committee. "To be quite honest, I didn't like that," Emily told us. "I missed him. I was used to having him around, and I'll really have to get used to it when he does go back to work."

Another spouse who made good use of this unexpected extra time was Millie, a staff trainer, and we mention her in order to point out that when we talk about a couple growing closer we don't necessarily mean spectacular changes in a relationship. Often just a quiet strengthening of a couple's intimacy is all that is required, or all they have time for. As Millie puts it: "Aaron would meet me after work and we'd drive home together, or if I had a spare hour, we'd go for coffee. Those are things I enjoy and we don't usually have time to do. Even then, we didn't have much time, but we got a lot of things talked out."

Respect: Part One

Fundamental to any marital contract is each party's respect for, and appreciation of, the other as an autonomous human being. Often a key part of this is respect for each other's space within the household. However, after a firing, many people attempt to compensate for their loss of self-esteem by trying to establish control over the children, the kitchen, the car, etc. We have already seen how much Kevin, Linda, Sharon and other spouses resented such intrusions. When speaking with us, they had absolutely no inhibitions about voicing the anger their partners' moves had provoked. In fact, they seemed to welcome an opportunity to let it all out. For example, Sharon had this to say about Ted: "He was out to manage the family, and it wasn't kind management. It was the 'how-to-create-roadblocks-and-hard-feelings' style of management. I could see what was happening, but I didn't have the skills or backup or any idea of how to break this pattern."

Linda added this about Ben: "He was trying desperately to be in control. One day he came home and said he was taking my car to Springfield for an appointment. He didn't ask—he just said it. But I was working that day, so I got into my car before he could and went to work. He came home that night and said he'd had car trouble and was an hour and a half late for his meeting, and it was all my fault because I'd taken my own car to my job."

And Kevin had this to say about Irene's involvement in the insurance brokerage he runs from their home: "It's true, I invited her to help me, and while my way of doing things may not be the best, it's the way I want it. But she was just not comfortable until things were organized to her satisfaction. Quite frankly, it was not only a problem in the business, it was a problem in our marriage for a good number of months."

Yet not all efforts to control a spouse are so deliberate or difficult to handle. Molly, the wife of the sober alcoholic and "poor unemployed manager," told us that she had, in effect, been preparing for the stress of Fred's dismissal for fifteen years. That is, for the first five years of his sobriety, she walked on eggshells, afraid that anything she might do would give him an excuse to start drinking again. But she finally realized that (*a*) if he did start, it would be his fault, not hers, and (*b*) she would be much more useful to him and herself if she adopted a tough love approach to their relationship. They learned to talk things out and, at the time of his dismissal, had enjoyed a long period of emotional stability.

However, the thirty-year reunion of Molly's college class was approaching. It was to be held in a distant city, and she told Fred she was going. "You should've seen his reaction!" she exclaimed. "I was devastated. I thought we were over all this insecurity and jealousy, but he was hoping he could get me so upset I wouldn't go. After all these years, he was trying to see if he could still control me. Being fired is what brought it on, and I really felt bad for him. But I also knew that if I didn't go, I'd be angry with him for the next couple of years, because these reunions only happen every five years, so I nipped it right in the bud. I said, 'If you're going to make yourself unhappy till I go, that's your choice, but I'm going. I know you don't want me to, but if you don't mind, I want you to take me to the train on Friday morning. I want you to kiss me goodbye and tell me to have a good time, whether you feel like it or not. And when I come home, I'd like you to meet me at the station, give me a hug and a kiss and ask me if I had a nice time.' And that was it. It was over."

Respect: Part Two

Molly got her hugs and kisses at the station and thereby maintained not only her own self-respect, but also the great respect Fred had developed for her over the previous fifteen years. In other relationships we encountered, the spouses reported that termination led their partners to greater and sometimes entirely new respect for them as people and for their interests and activities; and as often as not this coincided with new, personal growth on the part of their partners.

For example, Mary Ellen had long lived under the shadow of her husband, Derek, sales manager of a very troubled company. During the year and a half preceding his dismissal, the turmoil at the company seemed to be the primary concern of the household. In an effort to assert her own interests and remain on an even keel, Mary Ellen began doing volunteer work at a hospital. She also heard about a church-based renewal group, in which couples met to share their family experiences. When Mary Ellen asked Derek if he'd be interested in attending, he flatly said, "No, I'm not going to get into that sort of thing."

Derek was independent and generally preoccupied with matters other than his family. There was a fair bit of family strife after his firing, yet Mary Ellen was pleased to notice that he was now taking some interest in her volunteer work. Nevertheless, she was still surprised when he said he wanted to join her renewal group, and nothing could have prepared her for Derek's performance at the first meeting they attended. As Mary Ellen describes it, "When his turn to speak came around, he said, 'Well, I can tell you all tonight I am unemployed. I was the sales manager of such and such a company, and now I am out.' And then he began to really open up, speaking from his heart to me and everyone else." In his own quiet way, Derek had been paying attention to his wife and had decided to act, thus revising and enhancing their marriage.

Not everyone's story is (or needs to be) as dramatic as Mary Ellen and Derek's. If the original marital contract allows for change, the couple may not need to make more than minimal adjustments in order to cope with the dismissal. Clare and Les are a case in point. They had a few ups and downs, but nothing major, and when she summed up the experience for us, Clare had this to say about the fundamental adjustment she made: "When you have three kids and a busy house, half the time you're only listening to your partner with one ear. Something like this, though, can break a marriage, so you have to sit down and listen with both ears, and that's what I did."

Opening the other ear is not the most sensational coping method we could name, but sometimes that is all that's needed to keep the marital agreement intact.

Money

Clare and Les were fortunate in that they enjoyed eminently congruent goals and had no pressing money worries. Thus the dismissal crisis scarcely ruffled the equilibrium of their marriage. However, even couples who do have serious financial concerns can still work out ways of dealing with them during the crisis without jeopardizing their marriages. Indeed, shared financial planning can do a lot to lessen a couple's anxiety about the length of the job search and allow them to hold out until the best possible job is found.

Although it's not always easy, most couples are very good about this. The real trouble comes when money issues are actually expressions of deeper conflicts.

Back in the Limbo chapter, for example, we noted how anxious Angie was about her and Greg's finances. Yet as we talked further, she acknowledged that her real concern was that she did not want even a temporary revision of the financial portion of her marriage contract. She didn't put it that way, of course. What she said was "Money is not that much of an issue with us. We can survive on what we've got if we have to, but I don't want to have to. That's the bottom line. I want to have a little more than that."

In a somewhat similar vein, although Linda sees Ben's unsuccessful effort to start his own business as a basically positive thing, she still resents his many efforts to control the household, and she has chosen to fight him on the money issues. As she explained it to us, "We don't owe any money, and I'm not going to live as if we don't have a nickel. And I'm not going to eat Wonderbread, either." There and elsewhere, she spoke as if money and other issues were each isolated problems and not symptoms of her and Ben's fundamental differences over who is in charge of what. Moreover, even though she argues with him on such trivialities as what bread they eat and so forth, it does her no real good. Ben is still managing their money, and he retaliates by criticizing her spending on children's clothes (an area where she is actually quite frugal) and doing petty things like not insuring her car when he has two insured cars of his own.

Sharon and Ted have similar disagreements about money. Immediately after his firing, he insisted that they take a previously planned vacation, which Sharon wanted to cancel. The trip proved to be more expensive than anticipated, and shortly after they got back, their furnace broke. There was a costly twenty-first birthday gift for their elder daughter. They also needed a new car, and over Sharon's objections, Ted insisted on buying a brand-new, high-end model. Thus their financial strife continues, even though, as with the other couples we cited, they are in very little danger of ever learning firsthand what the term "poverty line" means.

In direct contrast to them, we have seen how delighted Sue Ann is to share her salary with her husband. The other parts of their marital contract are in pretty good shape, so the issue of money is not problematic.

Cynthia and Lloyd are still in an equally healthy financial situation. But as we noted in previous chapters, when he finally left the pharmaceutical firm where they had both worked, she had some deep-rooted doubts about his decision to become a consultant. He had already lined up enough work to keep him busy for six months and, on top of that, had received substantial severance pay. Still, Cynthia can't help looking ahead. As she expressed to us, "What happens after six months? He says the severance package gives us a good year. But I've placed that out of my mind altogether. Those are not funds to be spent. They're for when we're stuck. It is nice to have that money, of course, but life should go on as if we didn't have it."

The point to be noted here is that even though Cynthia can't shake the money anxieties brought on by Lloyd's dismissal, when they discuss the matter the issue really is money. When Linda and Ben quarrel about money, the real issues are the resentments and anger festering in other areas of their lives, which they have, for whatever reasons, chosen not to confront directly.

The Treatment of Children

Many spouses told us that their partners showed how unaccustomed they were to being at home during the day by becoming more critical of, and even angry with, the kids. An equal number of spouses reported that their partners became more involved with, and closer to, their children. Maggie saw both ends of the stick. As she reported earlier, her husband, Doug, a serious workaholic, eventually came to regret the time he had given to his former company and arrived at a new appreciation of his family, but this did not happen overnight.

At first, Maggie says, it was hell having him home all day, with the problem of the children often getting painfully entwined with other household issues that arose:

"He wanted to work, and I found that very difficult, because the kids wanted their friends over, and Doug said they would have to stay out in the backyard, because he couldn't stand the noise they made. With the humidity in July, keeping kids outside isn't the easiest thing to do when they've got a nice air-conditioned home. But at that time, Doug had a lot of anger toward me and the kids, so I had to keep them out, and he was also on my back because the house wasn't clean enough. He had probably never seen it in daylight, and suddenly he's after me to wash this and dust that. I was very angry inside, so the kids got shouted at a lot more than they did before. You know—'Be quiet, Daddy's working. Don't disturb Daddy.'

As we said, that situation didn't last, and we'll continue Maggie's story shortly. Also, we have devoted the next chapter to the complete range of children's issues.

Housework

Almost everyone we talked to seemed to have a unique arrangement in this area. At one extreme was Lisa, who said her husband had always done the cleaning and continued to do it after he had been fired. "Years ago," she explains, "he was in the Navy and they turned him into a neat freak. He has a high need for order. I often get a giggle out of it."

At the other extreme is Judith, a manager in a large corporation. From the day they were married, her husband had done his full share of the housework. After his dismissal, though, he flatly refused to do any domestic chores— probably, Judith guesses, because his self-image would be further damaged.

Somewhere in the middle is Vern. Seeing Harriet's enormous distress following her dismissal from the dairy products company, he made a special effort to be an even greater help around their house. "By the end, I was quite housebroken," he said jovially, "but it was all part of my strategy. I wanted her to get her mind off the situation. So I tried to do more of the housework than usual. I did the shopping, got the meals and did lots of the little things I usually ignored."

Then there is Gabriella, who told us: "We can be quite explosive, if I'm overloaded with my free-lance work, and I think Jason is not helping me enough. If he's been reading or watching TV and comes in and asks me why supper isn't ready, I explode. And he explodes when I've asked him to do too many chores in one day. So we explode and get it over with, usually pretty quickly."

The essence of the housework dilemma is that it's still a grossly undervalued occupation, and it can also be a power issue, especially in unbalanced relationships. That's why it was so refreshing to talk to spouses like Gabriella. On the whole, she and Jason have a nicely balanced marriage, and when they explode over some housework issue, you can be sure they are engaged in a quick fight between equals and not the latest skirmish in a prolonged battle for control.

Extended Family

In the course of a job search, a couple's extended families can be either a great help or a debilitating nuisance, and we have devoted chapter seven to this intricate matter. For now we'll just note a couple of interesting situations, beginning with a rather complicated case of family interference.

This is part of Kate's story, which we began in the Limbo chapter, outlining how she and Tim worked for a large farm machinery company from which he was clearly going to be dismissed:

Before the axe fell, Kate got an exciting new job in another city. Soon she and Tim were seeing each other only on weekends and she felt she couldn't talk about her new job while he was so miserable in his own. When she ran afoul of one of her new bosses, she yearned to discuss it with Tim, but didn't want to dump her problems on him, and when she learned she was pregnant, she felt she could not talk about that, either. When Tim was finally fired, they were both wrecks, and as if they needed any more pressure, his mother came charging onto the stage.

She was in an uncontrollable rage at the company that had fired her son. All Tim and Kate wanted to do was forget about the matter as quickly as possible, but she was constantly on the phone or at their house, rehashing and elaborating on her wrath. Moreover, she wanted revenge, and she was determined to get it.

Thus, while Tim and Kate were desperately trying to pull themselves together, they had to spend hours listening to his mother's rage and trying to talk her out of storming the company office. "She wanted to make the whole company and the guy who fired Tim hurt the way we'd been hurt and the way she felt she had personally been hurt," Kate says. "So every time Tim tried to pull himself up and out of all this, she was there to drag him back down."

Kate could see that Tim's mother's behavior was threatening his reputation and keeping him from his job search. But he interpreted his mother's hysteria as a show of unity, support and love. He did little to pacify her, and when Kate complained, Tim accused her of interfering.

As extreme as that situation was, it is still somewhat analogous to the debilitating help that many well-meaning families offer couples during a termination crisis. For example, immediately after her husband was dismissed, Leslie spent a great deal of time on the phone with his worried mother and other members of his family, who were constantly after her to get him out into the job market fast. This caused her to doubt Paul at a time when she was trying very hard to be supportive. Her own parents also called frequently, intending to be encouraging, but really only adding to the needless sense of urgency. Leslie had learned a lot about what to expect during the job search from Paul's brother, who had gone through a long period of unemployment; and her sister-in-law's frugality and general attitude during this period proved to be a great source of inspiration and encouragement for her.

Emotional and Behavioral Patterns

The changes that may occur here can be both significant and startling.

As a result of being fired, people who were once calm and cool may become quick to anger. Formerly positive and optimistic men and women can become depressed, and hitherto even-tempered people can suddenly become emotionally erratic. By the same token, the fired person's spouse can also become anxious and worried, critical, nagging and temperamental. One of the most notable examples of this is Maria. We began the Limbo chapter with her account of how Howard's job loss totally disrupted her household. She even resents the fact that she can no longer watch her favorite soaps by herself. In short, she resents any invasion of her space, and even though she knows full well that it makes her quarrelsome and her anger is seriously threatening her relationship, she feels she can do little about it.

Kevin just plain grew impatient with Irene's need to vent her anger at the insurance company. "I believe that's normal and a good outlet, and she had every right to expect a sympathetic ear from me," he said. "But quite honestly, after a month of non-stop anger, I didn't want to hear it any more. I was exhausted. Intellectually, I knew she needed to do it, but I couldn't see how this going over and over and over it again was improving things for her. I believe you have to put something like that behind you and get on with your life."

And Ian gave us this description of the wildly uncertain atmosphere at home during Victoria's job search: "I think most couples see the woman as being more emotional, more in touch with her feelings, and in a situation like this, I suppose her needs and the gender differences between you are magnified ten times. I was never sure where Victoria might be on any given day. Up? Down? How did the last interview go? I felt like I had to have my ear to the ground all the time. What's the situation today? Are things going well or not? Do I pump her up or just say everything will be fine? You have to be so closely in tune, ready to change the pitch at a moment's notice, and I found that very draining."

It's hard to predict what will set a person off in such situations, and many spouses told us how they tried to protect their partners by minimizing any outside aggravation that might provoke them. That was both thoughtful of them and a way of trying to maintain as much calm in their households as possible.

The spouses' partners may also try to shelter themselves from outside irritants. The extreme of this is withdrawal. They get so preoccupied with their concerns that they become distant from their spouses—present in body, it often seems, but no longer there in spirit. Sometimes it is only a temporary withdrawal, as in the case of Jennifer's husband, Stewart, in the months before his dismissal. And Millie told us that shortly before his firing, Aaron went into a brief, frenzied period of withdrawal in which he would sit up most of the night typing resumés and letters. It was totally unlike him, and he gave it up after a heart-to-heart talk with his exasperated wife.

Prolonged periods of withdrawal can leave a spouse hurt, confused, angry and wondering if he or she still has a marriage. For example, in the Limbo chapter we saw how badly Muriel and Karen were hurt by the way their partners excluded them from the job search. Karen's husband didn't even share the details of his severance package with her. And Muriel is showing some signs of going into a withdrawal of her own. That is, the rigors of her own work and the emotional strain of trying to regain contact with Harvey and get him to talk about his anger and break his long silences have left her feeling profoundly weary. Harvey, of course, is something of an extreme.

At the other extreme are partners who demand inordinate care and sympathy from their spouses. Fred's attempt to keep Molly from going to her reunion is a good example. She had the strength and experience to nip that stunt in the bud. But for many spouses in a termination crisis, it is often hard for them to tell where the extra support and love that their mates legitimately need ends and excessive pampering begins.

At one end there is Elaine, whose husband, James, suffered from depression. She knew that unless she gave every emotional resource she could muster to his recovery, she would no longer have a husband, a marriage or a house. At the other end is Sue Ann, who knew her husband as a friend long before they became lovers. After his firing he surprised her by descending into an uncharacteristic bout of self-pity, and her reaction was swift. As she explains it: "Sometimes when people feel like that, all they need is a kick in the butt, so I just flatly said, 'Buck, get off your butt and stop feeling sorry for yourself. You have everything going for you and there is absolutely no need for you to be down on yourself.'

"I guess I was basically saying, 'I have needs, too. I'm busy. I work long hours, and I can't be running around for you and running around for myself, too.' He was very, very angry, which I knew he would be. He'd done the same to me on previous occasions, and I was mad as hell, but then I realized he was right. And that's what happened when I did it to him. He went for a walk and came back and said, 'You know, you're right.' "

Again a couple's success in weathering a firing often depends on the strengths they bring into the crisis. However, some job seekers' despair is considerably more than a momentary fit of self-pity, and even the strongest spouses with the healthiest marriages spoke of needing to be careful not to get enmeshed in their partners' despondency. The danger, they saw, was in both partners getting sucked into a whirlpool of depression. This is certainly one way of being close, but it's not at all healthy, because neither party has the objectivity to be helpful to the other nor the emotional energy to help him- or herself.

The good news is that objectivity is not a remote ideal. The key to keeping the points we are discussing here in focus is a couple's capacity to renegotiate their marital contract and find new ways of accommodating each other's needs. There are five major objectivity-inducing techniques that will help you accomplish this. They are:

- Recognizing problems in your relationship
- Being flexible in the face of change
- Taking responsibility for your own actions in the relationship
- Communicating constructively with your partner
- Being genuinely committed to your relationship.

These are well worth pasting on your refrigerator, and we'll have more to say about them in the coping notes. We'll close this section by pointing out that sometimes it's the spouse who becomes depressed and the job seeker has to find ways of being supportive without sharing his or her spouse's negativity. During the course of Les's job search, Clare went through a temporary low, and he brought her out of it by staying up. That seemed to be his permanent condition, and he never revealed any of his deeper feelings about his firing. At times his reticence bothered Clare, but when she was depressed, his uplifting example was a source of great inspiration to her. As she puts it, "Eventually you have to go up, because there's no one down there with you."

If depression continues too long, setting a cheerful example may not be enough to revive a person's spirits, and professional help may be needed. But we found that in most cases, couples who could honestly share their feelings and provide each other with understanding and support were able to neutralize any depression before it took hold, and more than that, they increased their intimacy and closeness in the process. They had many ways of doing it. Gabriella and Jason, for example, found that with three kids running around the house, they talked most productively on the telephone, he at his outplacement consultant's office, she in her office at home. In this case, they were in fact listening with one ear, but it was quality listening.

Sexuality

Like the division of housework and money issues, the sexual relationship frequently mirrors a couple's communication patterns and reflects whatever degree of openness they enjoy. Couples who are working together to adjust to the dismissal and who discuss their needs openly with each other will often find their closeness and sharing reflected in the quality of their sex life. Couples who have trouble talking about their needs will probably distance themselves from each other sexually, as well. For some, sexual activity will continue, but the emotional closeness will be missing. Others will find themselves in a deepening mire similar to the one Karen and Gil are sinking into.

We have already mentioned their strife over money and housework and Karen's anger and bewilderment over his refusal to tell her about his job search. But that is almost in the past now. She is beyond anger and is withdrawing from Gil in a number of ways. "I'm afraid I'm getting into this horrible pattern," she says. "I come home, cook, clean up, do my motherly bit. Then I go upstairs, put on my pajamas and go to bed, hoping I fall asleep before Gil comes to bed. If he's not willing to share his job search and such with me, well, I don't want to share other things with him. If he can't share, I can't give, so our intimacy is gone. I really don't like it, but this is what I'm doing."

Lifestyle

There are two closely linked central issues here. One is the basic economic matter of curtailing the family's expenses during the job search and perhaps afterward if your partner takes a position with a lower salary. The second is the question of whether he or she will want to accept such a position, not so much because of the lesser pay, but because it would be a blow to his or her status and ego. Of course, nothing is ever that simple. For one thing, the job seeker's spouse's views must be considered. Angie doesn't want to make do with less, even during the job search. We have also seen how spouses like Cynthia and Olive, although generally in favor of their partners' entrepreneurial ventures, still can't shake their financial anxieties. Then there are situations where spouses can see that a less stressful position or a new line of work might be the best thing for everyone's peace of mind, regardless of the money.

Which brings us to the complexities of Mary Beth's situation. Her husband's firing dashed his lifelong plan to become president of the large transportation company he worked for. He was executive vice president before he was fired. One of his initial impulses was to make needless budget cuts at home, such as serving hamburgers to their guests, canceling their evenings out and not buying Christmas presents for their kids. Mary Beth met these moves with considerable tact, acknowledging the points he was making, but letting him know that while she was ready to make certain compromises, many others were out of the question. "Too many changes and I would have gotten very bitter," she says.

So their social life continued much as before and the kids got their presents. But that was only part of their problem. The primary one was, and still is, that Martin has absolutely no idea of what he wants to do next, although he can see that a job with much less pressure (and much less money) might be what he needs, and she has encouraged him to look in this direction. As she told us: "I am willing to step down. We have a very beautiful home, which is worth a lot of money. We could sell it and still live fairly well, although that's not what we've been working for all these years." In other words, as much as it might hurt, she is ready to make major lifestyle compromises, if that is what Martin needs.

In the case of Ross and Janice, he decided to return to school. She supported his decision, and their first step was to sit down and work out a long-term financial plan. "Janice has been earning more than me for some time," Ross explained, "but now she was going to be the sole support of our family. She didn't mind, but we'd never had a budget, because our combined incomes had always exceeded our spending. So now I've become a very firm believer in budgeting."

An even more heartening story comes from Cheryl and Glen, who are a prime example of how a truly communicative couple, if they share their dreams and are open to alternative values and lifestyles, can greatly expand their range of options. Ealier we noted how Cheryl eventually came to support Glen's dream of opening his own business, even though she was leery about the risks involved. She was certain that much of the risk could be avoided if they got into a field that was booming. Glen, however, insisted on buying into the paper-recycling business, which was in a slump, and this led to a major confrontation.

"We'd been married twenty years and had had some disagreements," Cheryl says, "but never an out-and-out fight. This time we did, and it was a dilly. Toward the end, he shouted, 'Where is your confidence in me?' And that got me thinking, 'Do I have respect for this man? Do I have confidence in him?' I realized I did, and that was when I got on the bandwagon and really became his partner."

The first year of the business, Cheryl adds, was extremely hard, but this feeling that she was a full partner in the venture paid off for her about eight months later, when Glen decided to buy yet another, related company: "When we got home that night, I put my foot down. I said, 'We are not buying that company. I'm not ready to do that yet. Let's work on this one.' He said, 'Okay,' and that was the end of it."

Job Search

A major source of conflict between job seekers and their spouses, we found, is that each partner may have a different way of approaching major projects. One may tend to work in a continual way, while the other might take a more episodic approach, doing one task and then relaxing a while before moving on to the next. Several spouses with the first tendency told us it drove them crazy to come home to find their partners watching television. One man told us that he was so upset with his wife's work-and-pause approach that, even if the TV was off when he came home, he would still feel it to see if it was warm. But his wife and the other work-and-pause partners probably felt perfectly justified in completing a series of phone calls or letters and taking a bit of a break before continuing with their job search.

The central point to note here is that, in households where the spouses were kept informed about the search, they were frequently able to make enormous contributions to it, sometimes simply by listening to their partners, at other times by offering advice and observations. Spouses with experience in the business world and whose partners valued their expertise were often asked for suggestions and perspective. And for many couples, the job search became another opportunity for sharing and closeness.

For example, the search gave Pat a rare opportunity to watch her husband at work. "It was exciting," she says. "Like when he was on the phone at home, calling his contacts. I was quite impressed and amazed and delighted to hear the authority in his voice, and to see him network and understand what it was all about. As his wife and his friend, I was extremely happy to see him growing in that dimension."

Roles and Responsibilities

A marital contract usually contains a spoken or unspoken agreement on each party's role in meeting the couple's economic needs. When a job loss occurs, the prospect of a sudden shift in roles can cause considerable conflict, depending on the couple's communications skills and flexibility.

For example, Lydia and Terry were an ambitious couple, each employed in the airline industry. Either salary would have provided a comfortable lifestyle for both, but they used their combined incomes to create a cushion of security that was important to them, especially Lydia. When Terry was fired, his ambition appeared to fade, and he seemed content to do the housework, cook and chat with their young daughter.

Lydia understood that he needed time to recover from his dismissal. But after a month of this, she began to fear that Terry liked being a househusband and was expecting her to be the family's sole wage earner. "That was definitely not part of the bargain between us," she says. "We do it together or not at all." Her first assault on the problem was a lot of nagging and shouting at Terry to get on with his job search, which he resolutely ignored. Luckily, their quarrels gave way to discussions of their respective fears, and Lydia finally understood that the firing had sapped Terry's confidence. She then was able to help him assess his skills and pump up the motivation he needed to get out into the job market.

We make it sound rather straightforward, but a lot of soul-searching and plain hard work goes into such successes. Elaine, for example, helped James devise a major career change. "But I didn't find him a job," she stresses. "I helped steer his energies. I just kept saying, 'You don't really like all the office work, but you do like servicing the customers who come into the office, so why not find out what their larger financial concerns are and be their consultant?' " And that is exactly what he did.

External Problems

As we noted in the case of Jennifer, a firing rarely occurs at a convenient time. Her husband's dismissal coincided with the death of her father, a stressful visit from her mother and a convention which she had to attend. Another case in point is Kate. When Tim was fired, her new job, her pregnancy and his mother's erratic behavior made it seem as if she'd never straighten out her life.

Then there is the case of Amy, who, after her husband Drew was fired a second time in a very short period, actually found relief from many external pressures. Drew's first job was a very high-profile, exceptionally stressful position in civic government. Amy believed in his work, and frequently acted as a sounding board for his thoughts and feelings. But, she adds, "I had my own stress with five children and the tedium of running the house and renovating. At the same time, he was coming to me with a ton of anxiety about work, and sometimes I'd think, 'If he tells me just one more thing, I'm going to go crazy,' because he was totally unaware of the situation at home. But I was freeing him up to do his work, which was important."

Drew was fired amid a barrage of media attention, which trebled the strain they were under. But it did help him find a similar job in another city. There, however, he soon found himself embroiled in another complex political situation. And while he was dealing with that, Amy was contending with several children's crises and trying to find a house. "We'd talk," she says, "and I would have nothing to say. It was all such grief. I would try to tell him about the strain of managing the children, but he couldn't handle any more."

His second firing came relatively soon, and this time he and Amy began to take stock of their lives. "We've never really had any time together," she told us. "People's lives get into such a jumble because of work and having a young family and so on, and a husband and wife, who were once very romantic, can hardly remember what it was like. They forget why they got together in the first place! So Drew and I have been making really good use of this time we have together now in the daytime, and it's fabulous. After he was fired the first time, we were so unnerved we couldn't enjoy it."

Previous Experience with Change

As Drew and Amy's experience so clearly indicates, surviving one crisis can make the next one easier to handle. Such crises (or tests, if you will) can come in many forms, including relocation and major career changes. Sue Ann, for example, was better equipped to handle Buck's firing because she had, a few years earlier, left a secure job at a sedate charitable foundation to start a new career as a theatrical agent. Moreover, in the course of her business life, she had seen many people fired for reasons that had nothing to do with their competence, so she was also intellectually prepared to cope with her husband's dismissal.

Above all, the long friendship that Sue Ann and Buck had enjoyed before their marriage gave them a firm base from which to face the crisis. This squares with our research findings, which suggest that mates who had been supportive of each other through difficult times in the past are able to approach a job loss with an underlying feeling of confidence in each other and the perseverance to see the crisis through.

Which is not to say it's ever been very easy. As we saw earlier, Fred's firing brought on a brief reversion to the type of controlling behavior that Molly had thought she'd seen end. But their having dealt with the trauma of Fred's alcoholism in the past gave them the strength and knowledge to deal with the job loss crisis immediately. Here, the experience of not just Fred and Molly but the entire family came into play.

Fifteen years ago, while Fred was at his AA meetings, Molly and the kids met with support groups for the spouses and children of alcoholics. Nor were the children excluded when Fred and Molly faced her battle with cancer eight years later. Consequently, though it has been rough at times, everyone has been able to face the current crisis with enviable strength. As Molly puts it: "If anything, there's more love now, and we've been able to meet it as a family. If you just go sailing along and don't have any of these crises, how do you know how much you're capable of handling? When I had my surgery, I found great support then, as well, both from my family and the cancer support groups. The experience you gain at those times can help you in any situation, and that's why this isn't as traumatic as it would be to a family that had just sailed right through and never faced any crises."

Relationships As a Whole

Conflict is all but inevitable when one or both partners' needs are no longer being met. The true test is the couple's ability to meet those needs by renegotiating their marital contract. The couples cited below were able to do so with varying degrees of success.

Good Relationships That Got Better

Despite some tough moments, most marriages described as good or close before a firing tended to become even stronger as husband and wife faced the crisis together and found understanding and support in each other.

Molly and Fred

We've just heard Molly say, "If anything, there's more love now." One sign of this is the way she and Fred handle one of the most common conflicts couples face during the job search: the spouse's need to know how it's going and the job seeker's reluctance to talk about it. "He pretty well does keep me up to date," Molly says. "I know who he's seen, who he's had lunch with. I think he feels that by sharing with me, he can make me feel better. But whenever he comes home and I say, 'What's new, dear?' he always replies, 'Nothing.' To me, that's a typical man, so I say, 'Well, who did you see?' and then I get all the answers. Once the initial 'nothing' is over, he's very communicative."

Leslie and Paul

We began this book with Leslie accompanying her shattered husband to our office. We've also shown you some of the doubts that plagued her during Paul's job search. But all in all, she says, the experience did bring them closer together, and when he finally found a job, they shared a marvelous feeling of relief and triumph: "He went out there and he did it. We did it. We dug deep and we made it!"

However, perhaps the most telling comment on their relationship came much earlier in the interview, when we asked how she felt about having a job while he was unemployed. "We never ever thought of him as not being the main breadwinner. That's strange. He always got up in the morning at the same time and got dressed as if he was going to the office and away he went on his job search. Perhaps we were playing games, like playing house, but he always went off. And although I was very glad I had my salary, I don't think in the eyes of the children, or in my eyes, he was ever diminished by not having a job."

Ian and Victoria

Before Victoria lost her job, she and Ian didn't give much thought to whether their marriage was good or bad. Exciting careers in the business world gave them a lot in common and added a certain competitiveness to their relationship. Ian described it this way: "After Victoria was fired, I felt like the breadwinner. You know, caveman brings home antelope. But we'd started off pretty well at the same point in business. I got ahead of her a couple of steps for a while. One time I was negotiating for a job and was offered an excellent package, but I still asked for a thousand bucks more. The guy asked why. I didn't tell him. I just said I needed it, and what I needed it for was it would put me a thousand bucks ahead of my wife. It was just a game, which we both enjoyed."

Victoria's firing put Ian clearly ahead, but he didn't gloat. "The firing was really rough on her," he said. "She'd always succeeded at whatever she did, and this made her feel like a terrible failure. She needed a lot of reassurance and a lot of hugs, and I tried as best I could to do that for her, though sometimes it was hard to know what I could do to make her feel better."

In the previous chapter, Ian described how the support Victoria received from him, family members and friends, made her realize how much these people meant to her. Her intense focus on career was cutting her off from them—especially Ian. They have since achieved a much better balance between their private and professional lives, and when Ian discussed the results with us, he began by saying, "Victoria tells me she finally feels married now. I think she and I bonded to each other a long time ago, but after our wedding, our careers took us in different directions. The firing helped us see that we were so intent on getting ahead, we were forgetting about us. We now realize that even if we get to be company presidents and have a big house and big cars and expensive vacations, it won't be any good if we can't share it. Big houses can burn down, big cars can crash and big jobs can be lost, and if you lose those things, what else do you have? Now we know how much we need each other. She's still hard-driven and so am I, but think we can now honestly say we're happy."

Stephanie and Alan

We must note that success does not always mean that everything is absolutely hunky-dory. Elsewhere we have mentioned Stephanie's doubts about why Alan was fired and her concerns about his drinking. His job search also caused her great pain. And now, after enduring all this, she is certain that he is terribly unhappy in his new job; and while she ignored the writing on the wall before his first firing, she can now see it quite clearly. Yet, despite all her trouble, and above everything else, she is extraordinarily proud that she and Alan did work through the crisis together. "We've talked about it a lot," she says. "It strengthened our relationship. There were no end of negative elements, but there were positive results, as well, because all of a sudden, instead of just taking life for granted, we had to be there for each other. So I think we're stronger in the sense that the picky things we used to argue about, we hardly mention any more. If he gets fired again, fine. I've now got all the strength I need to go through another job search."

Good Relationships That Began to Deteriorate

Some couples with good or at least satisfactory marriages before the dismissal found their marital contracts inadequate to the new order of things and had no idea of how to open negotiations for a new one.

Maria and Howard

The tragic thing here is that normally these two are superb companions, enjoying such quiet pursuits as tai chi, window shopping, gardening, driving around to look at other people's gardens and visiting construction sites to see the new houses. However, as we have noted, Maria cannot accept Howard's invasion of her weekday space. The resulting fights and his retaliatory refusal to share his job search with her, as well as his increasing impatience, have left her terribly afraid for her marriage. In short, she knows exactly what is happening but seems powerless to stop it. In the evening, rather than stay at home for another fight, she goes out and rides around on public transit, and she thinks he does the same. About the only time she feels close to him now is when he has an interview in a nearby city. She goes along and waits in a park or mall. And as he heads for his meeting, she likes to say, "I've got my fingers crossed for you."

Angie and Greg

The essential problem here is that Angie is terrified that one of the primary clauses in their marital contract is going to be radically revised. Greg has always been the main breadwinner, and she is afraid that his pursuit of a new career in the private sector will not be successful. But she cannot come right out and tell him this. As she puts it, she does not want to "shatter all his dreams." Therefore, rather than saying anything that he might take as criticism, she talks about the search in general terms and claims that she is being more realistic than he is, and he responds with exaggerated optimism. As a result, they keep talking around the central issue, while she becomes more frightened, miserable and angry.

Troubled Relationships That Improved

Firing almost inevitably brings a relationship's underlying problems to a head. Defenses are lowered, emotions run high and buried dissatisfactions erupt. In many cases, this is not a cause for overall alarm, because the strife impels the couple, for the first time, to admit that they do have problems and take the first steps toward solving them.

Maggie and Doug

Earlier in this chapter Maggie told us about Doug's anger toward her and their children. However, as he began to distance himself from his twelve-hour-a-day job, he started to appreciate the family he had badly neglected, and he and Maggie began to talk, rather than quarrel. In many ways it was the children who were the catalyst.

"He became a lot more relaxed," Maggie says. "He coached the girls' softball team, which was wonderful. The kids had a ball suddenly having Dad there, and he was able to give his time freely, which he hadn't been able to do before. When he was working, I think he was torn between wanting to do things like that, but feeling someone was paying him a salary, so he should be there whenever they needed him. He didn't change overnight. But I went back to work in September, and he's been driving the kids back and forth to school and sitting down at least two hours a night with their homework. I think he realizes that I don't have much time for myself now, and he wants to do more to help the family."

Sharon and Ted

From chapter two onward, we have been quoting Sharon in regard to her and Ted's money quarrels and his attempts to control her and the household. From the start, she took this to mean that he was acting out his insecurities, and she tried to make suitable allowances. But nothing was ever honestly discussed, her resentments and anger grew and Ted continued his thoughtless ways until there came a day when neither of them could ignore what had happened to their marriage.

Sharon described the crisis to us: "If you've gone through three or four months of your husband saying he's looking for a job and all you do is see him sleeping and going off here and there whenever he jolly well likes, you begin to wonder what's going on. I'm seeing nothing, yet he keeps saying he's doing something. So a lot of things erupted in June. He said I wasn't giving him any support in his job search, and I said, 'Well, I don't even know what you're doing. I'd be glad to hear what's going on.' He said he was re-evaluating his goals. I have a vague idea what that means, but he was doing all his goal re-evaluating by himself and not communicating any of it to me.

"Then in June he decided that his goal was to start his own business. Not only that, he'd also figured out how he was going to finance it. Without a word to me, he had decided that we were going to sell our house, put most of the money into the business and live frugally on whatever was left over. So I said, 'If you're going to live frugally, it looks as if I'm going to live on nothing, the way you're spending what money we've already got.'

"I didn't handle it very well, but I figured it was time to stop pussyfooting around and say, 'Hey, this isn't such a great situation.' What I was trying to say is, when somebody's re-evaluating his goals, it'd be nice if his spouse was let in on it, because any change will have a big effect on her life. It really bugs me. If you're a homemaker, everyone thinks you're flexible. They think nothing's really holding you down.

"Ted didn't want to hear any of this. He was ready to say this marriage was over and done with right then. But at that point, he went downtown and I drove off to the nursery school to get the kids. Ted and I then had a couple of very difficult days. But at the end of them, he did say he wanted to try and continue with me a bit longer, but I'd had enough. I said I wouldn't unless we took some marriage counseling. And that's what we're doing. Maybe we've taken the first step. I don't know. I like to think so."

Troubled Relationships That Continued That Way

Couples with relationships that were in serious difficulty before the firing and who lacked the ability to think objectively about their marriages tended to add the dismissal and its effects to their already lengthy list of complaints and incompatibilities. They continued to go around in the same old circles, their attempts at communication becoming mired in their efforts to change their partners, rather than themselves, and engaging in conflicts that never seemed to get resolved. We suspect that some of these marriages will move toward dissolution, though a few might continue to endure the disappointments of unmet expectations for quite some time.

Listen to three spouses in this situation:

Karen

Earlier in this chapter we saw how Karen no longer shares anything with Gil. Their intimacy is completely gone. Now, when she comes home at night, before entering the house she stops at the door and erases all expectations from her mind. Moreover, not long before we met her, Gil asked her to look up some data for his job search. A few months earlier this might have served as a small point of contact. At any rate, she got the data within minutes, but didn't pass it on to him. Why? "I'm tired of playing mother," she says. "I'm waiting for him to ask me for it." When we spoke with her, she had been waiting three days.

Muriel

In chapter two Muriel described Harvey's silence and his anger and her uncertainty about whether to leave him. She has coped to some degree by throwing herself into her research work and her M.B.A., but now she's tired. When we met her, Harvey was in an up mood, but that was no solace to Muriel: "What I'm wondering is, will he stay up? If he can, I'm sure he can find a job, because he does have the education, even though he's not in his twenties any more and he doesn't know exactly what he wants. But if he gets down again, he'll get angry, and we'll be back into that vicious circle. His money runs out in two months. I don't know what'll happen then."

Linda

Ben's frequent irritability and their quarrels about money and the children have left Linda as tired as Harvey and Karen are. She has tried to remain positive and gone out of her way to see the failure of Ben's business effort in the best possible light, but she is now beginning to wonder if it is worth continuing. As she puts it, "I think I expected more out of marriage. I guess I expected a lot from it. I never thought I would be living a solitary existence. I didn't think that I was the only one who was going to be looking out for me, or looking after me."

Imbalanced Relationships

In some instances, a dismissal will tip the give-get balance of a relationship so dramatically that one partner will end up doing all the giving and the other all the getting. This often happens when people are so debilitated by their dismissal that their spouses end up devoting themselves totally to their partners' needs, with no thought for their own. While such marriages generally endure, if the new marital contract does not at some point accommodate the spouse's needs, his or her dissatisfactions will probably emerge somewhere down the road.

Elaine and James

About the only exception to what we've just said is Elaine, and a clue to her strength and character is revealed in her account of her reaction to James's first firing. At the time she was a young socialite who had never known anything other than wealth and privilege. Yet when she realized just how difficult it was for James, she says, "It made me feel very strong, because it made me recognize that I'd been living in a dream. I'd been going to parties and wearing pretty clothes and decorating my house and not even asking how much things cost, and all of a sudden I felt like I'd been dropped to the ground. I looked around at all the nice things I'd collected over the years and I said, 'You spoiled, spoiled brat. All these years you've been expecting your husband to buy these things for you. There's got to be more substance to you than that.' "

As it turned out, there was. With absolutely no regrets, she unilaterally rewrote the contract in his favor.

Mary Beth and Martin

After his firing Martin underwent major surgery, and that and a number of other factors delayed the start of his job search for nearly a year. Now he doesn't know what he wants to do. Part of this is due to the blow his ego and confidence sustained when he was fired, and this has been exacerbated by a long period of recuperation. Although she might not like it, Mary Beth is ready to rewrite their marital contract to suit almost any direction he chooses to go, but waiting for him to decide is wearing her down.

"I tell him I'm losing patience, not at the fact that he doesn't have a job, but the fact that he hasn't any objectives, and he's not too happy. If he still wants to be a corporate man, or if he decides to go into business for himself, or if he turns around and says, 'I don't want to do anything, I want to retire,' fine. I'll be behind him. But all of this not knowing is dreadful. The first few weeks weren't bad. Neither were the first few months. A year was tolerable, but now it's over a year and a half. And you know, he does sort of try. Or at least he did. He wrote scores of letters and went to many interviews with headhunters and people like that, but now he seems to have given up. When I get home, I'll ask him, 'Did you go through the mail today?' 'Oh, yes.' 'Well, Martin, there are letters there and you didn't open them.' And he'll say, 'Well, you know what they'll all say.' And I'll say, 'You never can tell.' So I open each one and they're all the same, 'thanks, but no, thanks.' In something like this, you have to keep on trying and never ever get discouraged, but he is. It's like watching someone you love fade in front of you."

Marital Contracts Changed Because of Re-Evaluation

Job loss is a humbling experience and frequently followed by fairly intense self-examination on both spouses' parts. Often this leads to a shift in their fundamental priorities, values and behavior patterns. These may benefit not only the couple's relationship, but the entire family. Even in cases where they were not particularly dissatisfied with their previous situation, the new arrangement may be a considerable improvement in their life together. We offer two examples here.

Pat and Mark

In chapter two we saw Pat coming to terms with the powerlessness she felt as a homemaker when her husband was fired. In chapter three we saw her doing something about it by going back to school to learn a practical skill. And earlier in this chapter, she told how pleased she was to see her husband growing during his job search. This growth has carried over into his new job, the acceptance of which was a mutual decision on their part. "We had the feeling that maybe he should be in a slightly smaller company," Pat says. "He's not terribly political or terribly aggressive, and he doesn't have a great need to be president. We talked about that and it gave him a clearer idea of what he should be looking for, and he pretty well got it. He was on the pure technical side before. His new job is much more administrative and people-oriented, which is more him. He's grown in so many ways, and that's nice to see."

Kate and Tim

Kate is the woman with the enraged mother-in-law. At the time of Tim's firing, she was also trying to cope with the excitement and strains of her new job, her pregnancy and the devastation of Tim's situation. He did finally begin to mount a thorough job search, but she still didn't tell him she was pregnant. She felt that the sudden burden of a family at this time would be more strain than he could handle, especially with his mother still phoning, visiting and venting her rage.

Luckily, Kate's mother sensed that all was not well and offered them a weekend alone at the family cottage. It was there that they came face to face with a central problem in their marriage: all they had ever had in common was their former jobs—the sale of farm machinery. "At the cottage," Kate says, "we didn't know what to say to each other. That had never happened to us before. And I realized that whenever we'd talked before, it had been about tractors. We had never really taken time to get down to the basics of what our relationship was founded on. When I met Tim, my dad had a stroke. It was a very difficult time, and I just said to Tim, 'Look, if you want to see me, I'm going to be at my parents' house. You're welcome to come down with me and sit in the living room while I'm in my dad's bedroom.' And that's pretty well how our courtship went. We never had a normal beginning. My dad died and we got married and then there was all this traveling we did for the company. So we never had a chance to sit down and have whatever a normal kind of beginning is for a couple.

"Then, when we were at the cottage, all of a sudden we couldn't talk about our work together, because it wasn't there anymore. I couldn't talk about my problems at work because that would be dumping on him, and Tim had no work to tell me about. And he didn't want to talk about his mom to me because I would explode. So I wondered, after a year and a half, what had we come to? So I thought, we'd better pull something together here. It was really hard, but I did finally tell him about the baby. I had to. I was falling asleep at three in the afternoon every day, so I had to explain why. And he was thrilled. He said, 'Why did you wait? I'm not worried about getting a job.' And that was really the first time that we'd confronted his firing. The baby gave us the opening to talk, and we started going through everything. We started saying things and talking them through, just like real couples do."

COPING

» 1. If, as a result of his or her firing, you and your partner are having difficulties, you might think about your relationship in terms of the five objectivity-inducing techniques we mentioned earlier in the chapter. They are:

- **Awareness.** The crucial first step toward solving any problems you and your partner may have is acknowledging that these tensions and dissatisfactions do exist.

- **A sense of personal responsibility.** Taking a good hard look at your own behavior and examining its impact on your partner will give decisive insights into your contributions to the problems, which is another important step toward solving them.

- **Constructive communication.** Couples who can talk openly about the dismissal, the job search, their feelings and needs and their relationships, as a whole, are the ones most likely to improve their situations. They listen carefully to each other and work hard to understand what their mates are saying and feeling. They are also willing to make themselves vulnerable by revealing their feelings, and they look for ways to say things in a manner that is not threatening, harsh or overly aggressive. This, however, does not rule out a good air-clearing fight, as long as you don't get stuck there.

• **Flexibility.** Flexible people spend their energies not in regretting, but in adapting to, change, "discarding what has been in the past for that which is more appropriate to the future." They are more willing to compromise and make trade-offs, so that the needs of everyone in the family are respected and no one feels neglected or abused. Don't waste your time longing for a return to the way things used to be. Expect change and try to make it work to your advantage.

• **Commitment.** Even if you and your partner have all of the above skills, you must also be truly committed to making your relationship work. In short, you have to want it.

» 2. If any of these five factors are missing from your relationship, you might think about how you can develop and apply them. Start small. Concentrate on your own behavior and work on doing one specific and manageable thing differently.

» 3. We are not, of course, saying that you have to meet every one of your partner's needs. The object is to define these needs as precisely as possible and then in a calm, rational manner go on and discuss whether you can or want to meet them.

» The quotation and these concepts are from "Marriages that Endure", an article by the clinical staff of the Marriage Council of Philadelphia, which appeared in the journal *Human Sexuality*, Vol. 19, No. 4, April 1985. We are also greatly indebted to Dr. Edward P. Monte's article "The Relationship Life-Cycle," in *Treating Couples: The Intersystem Model of the Marriage Council of Philadelphia*, edited by Gerald R. Weeks, Brunner/Mazel, New York, 1989.

» 4. By the same token, think about how specific you are being about your own needs. Again, to take a very simple example, snapping at your partner and angrily saying things like "You might at least pitch in around here" will only get his or her back up. One woman we interviewed was constantly furious with her husband and was always snapping at him about the housework. But then she thought about what this was achieving and one morning very casually mentioned that she had a rough day ahead and asked if he would have time to do a specific task for her. He did it without a complaint.

» 5. When you do modify your behavior, monitor the results. Don't expect huge changes in your partner, but pay close attention to positive effects. This will help you learn what works and what doesn't.

» 6. For the sake of clarity, we have simplified the five factors, but they are rarely simple or easy to achieve, so don't feel badly if you find that you and your partner can't bring about changes by yourself. Sometimes it takes the help of a marriage counselor to sort out a relationship's many complexities and intricate dynamics.

» 7. Your public library is full of good books that may be useful to you at this time. To help get you started, we have included a list of further reading at the end of this book.

» 8. If you aren't getting enough information about your mate's job search and want more, talk to your partner. That is, express things in terms of your own needs and peace of mind. Make it clear that you are not demanding a report card.

» 9. As a couple, try to arrange some private time together just to enjoy each other's company and get away from the job search for a while. This need not be anything exotic, although that's nice, too. Sometimes all that's needed is a refreshing walk every other night, an occasional movie or maybe drinks and a hamburger at a cozy spot.

Chapter Six

The Two of You and the Kids

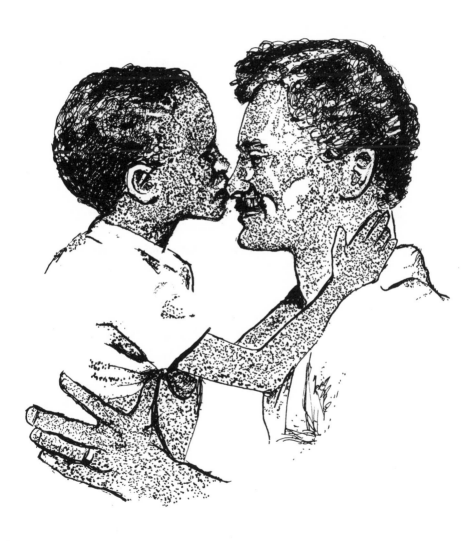

Termination brings many worries about the children, the most immediate being how to break the news to them. Depending on their ages, this will require figuring out how to tell them so they understand; how to tell them so they will not be frightened or overly worried; how to answer their "why?" questions, even if you and your mate are not precisely sure why the job loss occurred; and how to respond to their emotional reactions when you may be extremely upset yourself.

For many people who have lost their jobs, the fear of appearing to be a failure in their children's eyes is considerable. Their spouses are usually acutely aware of this and anxious to do whatever they can to prevent that worry from becoming a reality. Frances and Nick, for example, told their children that his leaving the insurance firm where he had been a high-level manager for twenty years was a mutual agreement between him and the company. This was not exactly true. He had wanted to stay, but the new owners insisted on revising his contract in a way that he could not accept. Similarly, Lisa and Cliff and many other parents we encountered took great pains to ensure that their kids understood the difference between a downsizing and an old-fashioned firing.

However, the greatest concern for most spouses was that their kids should not suffer from their mates' dismissal, and they worked hard to hide their own worries and maintain their children's lifestyles. Agnes is only one of dozens of parents we could cite in this regard. Says she: "My daughter went to camp as usual. Her swimming lessons and dancing continued. So nothing really changed for her. Earl and I had to sacrifice for it, but I think it was the best thing in the long run, because she would've been devastated had she not been able to do these things with her friends. That's something I learned from my neighbor and her husband, who went through a firing last year."

On the whole, the spouses we spoke with did succeed in keeping their children's lifestyles and activities as close to normal as possible. What struck us, though, was that many of them believed their partners' firing had had no impact on their children at all. Yet as we went on talking, they recalled comments and small incidents suggesting that while their kids might not be saying much, they certainly had serious thoughts and feelings about the dismissal.

For instance, one woman told us how, after listening to her and her husband talk about his impending termination over a month or so, their very young son came downstairs one night with his piggy bank and tearfully offered to donate it to the family finances.

They thought it was cute. But the boy was clearly very worried, and in this, he was by no means unique. Moreover, children's termination worries are not restricted to the family finances.

In fact, it is quite unrealistic to assume that children will not be affected by something that so profoundly affects their parents, or to assume that they will not experience any negative effects. The realistic course is to try to anticipate these effects and enlist the children's cooperation in dealing with them in a way that will minimize their negative impact. The big stumbling block here is that most parents are so determined to keep their kids' lives as normal as possible that unless the kids' behavior is extremely disruptive, the parents tend to assume the firing has made no impact on them. Parents may also be so preoccupied with their own concerns that they miss vital clues to their children's feelings.

On the other hand, there are parents who believe it isn't a bad thing for their kids to go through rough times occasionally. In their view, crises help them grow as people and as members of a family, testing their ability to deal with life and teaching them to do so.

A related question is the overall message that termination imparts to children. Having grown up in a time when a good education, hard work and loyalty to the company were enough to ensure job security, some parents are now wondering what values and work ethic they should pass on to their kids, not only to help them survive, but also to help build their character.

One woman told us that after her husband was fired, their daughter questioned the value of continuing her university studies. They said she definitely should, and she bluntly countered with the words, "Where did it get you, Dad?" And Rosemary had this to say about the current employment climate: "It doesn't matter how hard you try any more, there are no guarantees, and that's what I've struggled with most. I really wonder what the kids have to look forward to. It's a big turnaround from growing up thinking the world is your oyster, the way we did when I was in college."

The other side of that coin is the parents who felt that the firing was a timely lesson for the children, in the hard fact that anyone, at any time, is vulnerable to termination. For example, Molly told us that she was happy to hear her twenty-year-old son repeating the old business adage, "the closer you are to the top, the nearer you are to the door." And Pat said she and her husband were pleased to see that his firing gave their young children an awareness they would not have had otherwise. "We've had family conversations about the possibility of losing a job and the importance of getting an education. They now have some sense of how tough it is out there."

We could quote many other parents to that effect, but it can also be tough at home during a termination crisis, and that is what this chapter is about. We have divided it into three parts: children's possible initial reactions to a dismissal, their reactions over time, and their reactions to a parent's job search.

Initial Reactions

It's important to remember that children's responses to a dismissal will vary considerably, according to age, personal characteristics, life circumstances and family dynamics.

Shock and Disbelief

We'll immediately contradict ourselves by saying that initial shock and disbelief are an almost universal response, hitting children of all ages. Here are only three of many possible examples. Describing the reactions of her three adult children, Molly said: "They were all the same—'How can they do this to Dad?' 'How can they be so ruthless and so heartless?' " Recalling their daughters' reaction to Harriet's dismissal from the dairy products firm, Vern said: "Both of them work in marketing, so they knew even better than I did the value of what Harriet had been doing. The firing utterly astonished them." And speaking about her young children, Stephanie said: "I think over time, they thought it was great—Dad's home every day. But that first day, it really upset them. They found it hard to understand. They kept asking 'Why?' and 'How come?' and saying things like 'They can't do that.'" The key word is *they*. For children of all ages, their parents are twin cornerstones of the universe. It's inconceivable that an employer could no longer want them. Thus, for very young children and teens, as well as adult offspring, a parent's termination may be simultaneously devastating in itself and their first glimpse of their parents' vulnerability.

Confusion and Anxiety

Children who are too young to grasp fully what is happening may sense their parents' tension and begin wondering what changes will result. However, they may not make these feelings obvious, or they may not have the skills to verbalize their fears. Instead these may be revealed in more subtle ways, through play, art work, cryptic sentences, occasional questions and such regressive behavior as bed-wetting and baby talk. In short, unless a parent is paying close attention, it's often easy to miss a young child's concerns.

Occasionally, though, there can be no mistaking what's on a child's mind. The boy offering his piggy bank is a good example. We also heard of a boy whose anxiety prompted him to try to earn some money for his parents by setting up a lemonade stand in the street in front of their house. On a much more serious note, one man told us that, several weeks after his wife had lost her job, their nine-year-old daughter suddenly asked him, "Daddy, are you and Mommy getting a divorce?" Not wishing to worry their kids, the man and his wife had been in the habit of going into their bedroom and shutting the door when they wanted to talk about the firing and the job search. The nine-year-old could tell something was up and had interpreted her parents' unusual behavior as a sign of the worst thing she could imagine.

And Pat has this story: "We talk about a lot of things at dinner, and one night the topic was the importance of getting a good education so you can choose what you want to do. Ages ago, my husband must have mentioned that when he was a boy, he had wanted to be a doctor. Anyway, while we were talking, our youngest, who was six, suddenly leaped up from the table crying, and went around and sat on Mark's knee and said something like, 'I really wish you could have been a doctor so you could've done what you wanted to do and not got fired, Daddy.' We were all quite tearful and quite struck by what he'd said. I guess the situation had been percolating through his mind. It's often very hard to tell how worried kids are."

Why?

This is an important question for children of all ages, because the answer can lead to two unsettling conclusions. If the company was wrong in firing Mom or Dad, it means that they can strike arbitrarily. A sudden realization of this may provoke a sense of injustice, vulnerability and outrage. Yet as uncomfortable as these feelings may be, they are preferable to the alternative, which is a suspicion that if the company was right in firing him or her, Mom or Dad might not be the people the kids thought them to be.

Leslie says one of the reasons she was so angered by Paul's firing was that it disturbed not only him and her, but also their son and daughters, who were in their late teens and early twenties: "In their eyes, I think, their father had gone down a notch. And that was scary for him, because the kids were saying to him, 'Dad, what happened?' They're old enough to know that these things have a reason and they wanted him to give them a specific answer so they could in turn give him the benefit of the doubt, and he knew that."

Tears and Anger for the Fired Parent

Vern told us that his adult daughters were furious about their mother's dismissal: "They kept saying things like, 'You're too good for them, Mom.' 'You're better off not being in that corrupt place.' "

Leslie also saw hurt and anger in her daughters' eyes. "It hit the youngest one particularly hard," she told us. "She tends to be quite verbal, and she was always saying, 'If I were you, I'd go down there and tell them this, this and this.' I mean, she went on and on until Paul found himself almost defending the company, which was quite funny."

Maggie and Doug had to deal with similar hurt and anger in their ten-year-old. "She expressed it," Maggie says, "by saying such things as 'He was a mean guy where you used to work at, wasn't he?' and 'He's the man who doesn't like you any more, Daddy.' Doug had to sit down and explain that it was not a matter of liking or disliking but a business decision, which was hard for her to understand."

Finally, in one of the more extreme cases of anger we encountered, a woman was rudely fired by her new boss from a job she'd held for twenty years. The woman was surprised by neither the firing nor her insulting severance package. More than anything, she was happy to be out of the place, and she was quickly hired by a rival firm. However, the woman's son was so enraged that he browbeat her into suing her former employer. She won, but only her son got any satisfaction from the verdict. To her, the lawsuit was simply a nasty experience she would rather not have endured.

Tears and Anger at the Fired Parent

Most of the hurt and anger we heard about was the result of children's sympathy for their fired parents, but we also found that a considerable number of children greeted termination with grief for the times their fired parents had not spent with them because of work. They appeared to re-experience the sadness and anger they had felt when Mom or Dad had missed their birthdays and holidays and special baseball games and musical performances. Consciously or unconsciously, they felt that they had sacrificed a lot to the parent's job, and all for naught. Mom or Dad was fired anyway.

Some kids in this situation simply nurse their grief. Others direct their hurt and anger toward the company. And there are a few who are angry at the fired parent.

The most blatant example of this is Elaine's children, who are in their twenties and early thirties. When Elaine told them about James's second firing, one of them said, "Oh, my God, Mom, he's not doing that to you again, is he?" With the exception of the youngest, they each said much the same thing. It sounds cruel, but it's important to understand that for most of their lives, James was usually too busy at work to spend much time with them, and what time he did give was so fraught with hurts and mutual resentments that it was unpleasant for everyone. In addition, James's career ups and downs meant he could not pay their way through college. Most children can, of course, overcome such setbacks and worse, but Elaine and James's two eldest kids never have. They blame him for their many personal failures. And now that James has recovered and is doing very well in his business, he sends them large, monthly checks, as if this will recoup their respect. So far it hasn't.

Worry

Termination and its effects can cause children of all ages to worry about their parents and themselves.

Children who are still living at home have two basic worries. One is the fear of relocation, which can affect even the most adaptable youngsters—and any parent of teenagers will know how disheartening they will find the prospect of leaving their school and friends behind. Clare, though, gave us an interesting twist on this. Her son is in his first year at a university in another city. For a while it looked as if her husband might get a job in that city, which the boy didn't like at all. He was hugely enjoying living away from home and knew that if his parents did move there, he would have to live with them.

The other basic worry is that their lifestyle will have to change. This concern affects even younger children. For example, Stephanie's youngsters were overjoyed when Alan finally found a job. "It was the beginning of December," she says. "Christmas was coming up, and a month or so before that, we had sat down and said to them, 'Now, you know if Dad's not working, you might get only one gift each,' and I think it was hard for them to deal with."

Children in their early twenties can also worry about finances, their concerns ranging from being able to continue their education to whether there will be enough money for planned weddings and such. But the most concerned group will usually be the teenagers, with their endless need for the clothes, haircuts, music and countless other things that signify membership and acceptance in their peer group.

After Percy's first dismissal, he and Angela warned their teenagers that there might have to be some financial cutbacks. As things turned out, Percy got a job before these became necessary. But now that he has been terminated again, there is no question that sacrifices will have to be made. "I don't know how much of it will sink in," Angela says. "When they showed us their Christmas lists last year, after Percy and I had warned them about hard times, it did not seem as if they understood what was going on."

And here we have the crux of the matter of teens and money: they will worry about continued funding, but in most cases, once they see that their lifestyles will be going on much as before, they appear to forget there is any money problem at all. Valerie is quite philosophical about it and even somewhat amused. "The young one is funny," she says. "I said, 'Daddy's not working now. He's looking for another job.' She just said, 'Oh, yeah, fine.' You know, that age group. They don't know how life goes on. But my fifteen-year-old stepdaughter—she wanted to know if she'd be able to stay in her music lessons. I told her not to worry, and she seemed quite relieved. We did, though, try to impress upon her that we'd have to pull in to some degree, but she seems to have forgotten, because she's always wanting this and that, like all teenagers do, I guess."

For her part, Jane was rather taken aback by how nonchalant her children appeared to be when they were assured that there would still be money for their university tuition and other expenses: "They took it completely for granted. I think they just assumed it was part of their right in life." Similarly, Cynthia was amazed by her stepchildren's apparent indifference to Lloyd's dismissal. "I expected some reaction, but there wasn't any," she says. "I really think what it came down to was, 'Well, as long as there's no change and we can still go to school, there's no real impact on us.'"

But children are not entirely self-centered and they also worry about their parents. For example, Vern and Harriet's daughters knew how badly their mother had been devastated by her firing. "So one would call from California every morning," Vern said, "and the other would call from Chicago every night. They kept it up for months, till Harriet got that consulting job and began to feel better about herself."

We heard many such stories, all of them demonstrating not only how much children can worry about their parents, but also how extremely sensitive and thoughtful they can be.

Embarrassment

With today's often very generous severance payments and most parents' determination to avoid curtailing their children's activities unless it is absolutely necessary, it's quite understandable that many kids will not worry for long about the financial implications of a parent's dismissal. But children can react very strongly to other things. For example, the firing itself can cause some kids to feel very uncomfortable, even embarrassed. In the case of Mary Ellen's youngest child, it was simply a matter of the boy not knowing how to explain his dad's termination to his friends. "I told him to say his father was a very good sales manager and he was very happy to be gone from that firm," Mary Ellen says.

That was all it took to end the problem. Angela, on the other hand, didn't realize there was a problem until the day, a few weeks after her husband's second dismissal, when one of their eldest son's friends came to the door. "The boy," Angela says, "casually asked, 'Doesn't your dad have a car?' and Robin said, 'Sure he does. It's just in the garage.' He wasn't able to say we no longer had the company car."

The key to forestalling such embarrassment is giving children some suggestions on how to tell others about the dismissal, and, in most cases, a frank and open approach to the firing on the part of the parents. For instance, Jane told us that her children's cool response to her husband's job loss was also a reflection of his own attitude, which was completely free of embarrassment. To take just one example, when the kids came in with their friends, Gavin didn't slink away and hide in another room as if he were ashamed to be home during the day. He stayed where he was and chatted with the young people. Now and then, the conversation turned to his firing and job search, which he discussed in a totally matter-of-fact manner.

During our interviews, we also learned that children often found comfort in being able to compare notes with a contemporary who also had an unemployed parent.

Agnes was only one of many parents who told us this. As she put it: "I don't think Sonja was too touched by the firing. We were able to keep our spirits up, and also her best friend's father had been let off, too, so she had someone to share the experience with."

But in those first days after a dismissal, the fired parent and his or her spouse can be quite devastated, and although they intend to remain open and rational, the situation can overwhelm them, with the result that the children sometimes end up suffering the kind of embarrassment that comes from seeing their parents suddenly diminished. Earlier, Leslie described how Paul's inability to give their children a precise reason for his dismissal was frightening, because he didn't have one. They could not understand this, and it became an increasingly vicious circle, with the kids persisting in their questions and their father desperately trying to answer them and to erase the doubt he saw in their eyes. "He was being extremely honest and open," Leslie says, "but they couldn't see that, either, so he ended up feeling he'd let not only himself down, but us, as well."

Another example of good intentions going badly awry comes from Amy, who got a frightening surprise during the political turmoil and media attention that accompanied her husband's first dismissal. "It never occurred to me to be concerned about the effect on the kids," she says. "In fact, I was thinking it would be good for Irv, our seventeen-year-old, to see how resilient his dad was, but I think it panicked him. I mean, Drew was understandably tense and edgy, but he was coping wonderfully well, considering all the uproar that was going on, but Irv must have seen it as panic, and it frightened him, sending him into a tailspin. Maybe he suddenly saw how difficult it was to be an adult. Anyway, he was depressed and seemed to be in a fog. It lasted a couple of months, and we started seeing a family counselor, who's helped us a lot."

Taking the long view, the facts that Mom or Dad is a mere mortal and that being an adult is often very difficult are things all kids must learn sometime. From our experience, the tendency is for most families to ease gradually into variations of the patterns of behavior that prevailed before the firing. If the fired parent continues to have image problems, it's usually for reasons other than the fact that he or she was fired.

Reactions Over Time

Everyone reacts to a crisis in his or her own way. Thus, consciously or unconsciously, both parents and children perceive that one of their primary tasks is to make the dozens of necessary adjustments to one another's behavior and maintain some semblance of the order and balance that the family enjoyed before the axe fell.

Occasionally, children can be too delicate about someone's feelings. For example, Molly's married daughters took to asking her how their father was. "They were afraid he wouldn't want to upset them by telling them how he really felt," Molly says. "They seemed to have forgotten that we do express emotions in this house, so I said, 'Daddy's fine, but why don't you ask him yourself?' Fred wasn't afraid to say he was maybe a bit depressed, or he wished things would hurry up and start moving for him."

At the other end of the scale, Jennifer found that considerable delicacy was called for during the six months of Limbo that the family endured before her husband, Stewart, was dismissed. "He was under great stress at work." And at home he often seemed so preoccupied, it was as if he wasn't really there. All that I and the children could do was be there for support and not make waves," Jennifer says.

She makes it all sound rather straightforward, but it wasn't, and the stress completely overwhelmed one child. "Robert did very poorly in school," Jennifer recalled. "He was sick constantly, and getting terrible headaches at school. I think a lot of it was stress and tension that he was keeping inside. He's very considerate of me, and I suspect he didn't want to tell me about what was bothering him and have me worrying about him and his father. Although, of course, I was worried about him." Even though Jennifer was worried, it was only afterward that she fully realized the connection between the boy's behavior and Stewart's impending dismissal.

Several other spouses told us that during their partners' job searches, they also missed vital clues to their children's feelings; and this is the basis of our belief that in many instances parents are too preoccupied with their own stress to link changes in their children with the termination. Another possibility is that these changes often take months to develop and are, therefore, very easy for a parent to miss. Sharon witnessed one such drama, and her testimony is notable for two reasons. First, it is a very good illustration of how long it takes some children to adjust to the changes in family dynamics brought about by a firing. Second, it's an excellent example of how hard it can be for a preoccupied parent to interpret a child's behavior.

In the last chapter, we related how Sharon and Ted are now in counseling in an effort to save their marriage. The root of their crisis was the year or so before Ted's dismissal, when the merger of his company with another almost doubled his workload. On the rare occasions that he came home in the early evening, he was too exhausted to be involved with his wife and daughters, and they adapted to this. Then, when he got fired and was home most of the day, the girls continued to treat him as if he were invisible, which both hurt and astonished him.

"Before he was fired," Sharon says, "he'd come home and we'd ignore him. That's the way he wanted it. So after he was fired, it took the girls a couple of months to realize he didn't want them to ignore him any more. Our six-year-old would actually hide from him. She just didn't know what he would do."

It was a good seven weeks before the girl accepted him as part her life again and stopped hiding from him. During this period, her schoolwork suffered; and besides the radical adjustment to their routines necessitated by Ted's mere presence at home, she and her sisters also had to deal with the new financial realities of cutbacks in their clothes buying, ballet lessons and other activities.

Nothing in Sharon and Ted's situation is settled yet, but the eldest daughter, who is ten, appears to have landed on Daddy's side and become quite bossy in her attempts to keep the other two girls quiet for his sake. There are two possible explanations for this.

One is that it could merely be her way of adapting to the new, Daddy's-home-now regime. The second is that she may have picked up some of the unresolved marital tension between Sharon and Ted and, as many children will do when they sense that things aren't right, may be trying to maintain a measure of balance in the family. Sharon and Ted seem to think they have managed to keep their deeper troubles from their daughters, but it's hard to imagine how the girls could have failed to notice and be affected by their parents' tension.

In the case of Karen and Gil's children, there is no question that they know their parents are having difficulty with their relationship and that the kids are doing everything they can to save it. The children are twelve and seventeen. Before Gil was fired, the younger was close to her father, while the elder was closer to his mother. Since then, the family dynamic has turned completely around. The central problem was the growing estrangement of the parents. But Gil was on the kids' backs, as well, and one of the first clues to the new order of things came when the daughter made some comment about not going to college because a person doesn't need a degree to make a lot of money. "Gil came down on her pretty strong," Karen says. "He also gave her the old lecture about how, if you work hard at school, you can't help but be a success, and she just looked at him and said, 'You're a good one to talk.' Which really hurt my husband."

Another significant confrontation also involved education. The elder child, who was in his last year of high school, dropped a couple of peripheral courses in order to take a part-time job so that he would be sure to have enough money to go on to college. Gil either failed to see why the boy had done it, or he knew perfectly well that his son was concerned about the family's finances, and Gil felt badly about it. At any rate, he berated the boy as if he had dropped the courses out of laziness or was ignorant of the value of a thorough education.

Unlike his younger sister, the boy did not fight back or try to hurt Gil. Instead he is making a great effort to understand Gil's point of view and trying to get his mother to be equally empathetic. At the same time, the girl gives Karen a hand with the housework and makes no secret of her belief that since Gil is home all day, he should be doing these chores. If anything, Karen seems bemused by this turnaround, which has seen the son, who was never close to Gil, become his biggest advocate in the family, while the younger one, who was once Gil's favorite, is now very much anti-Dad. Karen doesn't seem to grasp fully that her children are working hard to keep the family balanced and intact.

To be sure, this was probably not a conscious decision on the children's part, but at some level they must have realized that if they both sided with Mom, the three-against-one situation would have tipped the already precarious balance of the family dynamic. Similarly, they must have also figured that if each aligned with the parent he or she was closest to, the result would have been an equally dangerous emphasis of Karen and Gil's differences. Ultimately, of course, the kids are powerless. If Karen and Gil don't start putting their own balancing act together soon, it is all but inevitable that the pressure on the children will continue to mount and their own relationship will continue to deteriorate.

So far we have tended to emphasize the more spectacular, and generally negative, ways in which a firing can affect children. We feel it is necessary to point out this possibility because so many parents can't see any effects. But we would be remiss if we did not place equal emphasis on the fact that we also found many positive results of having Mom or Dad around more.

An unqualified positive was reported by Ross and Janice. After his dismissal, Ross decided to return to school and did much of his studying at home, while after she was let go from her job, Janice was at home much of the day because she was pregnant. "So the kids have had a full year with both their parents, and it's been good for them," Ross told us. "They had the best of both of us, because we kept our nanny and their old routines."

We could fill the next five pages with similar stories from other parents who reported positive experiences. A dismissal is often a real opportunity for parents to tidy up or strengthen the bonds with their children, and in certain circumstances a dismissal can indeed be very beneficial.

Besides the couple already noted, we can also point to Jennifer and Stewart. His remoteness from his kids in the six months preceding his dismissal was not that unusual, because of the long hours he spent at work. Thus, when his daughter was ready to learn to drive, he went out with her only a few times. His son's turn to learn, on the other hand, coincided with his dismissal, and Jennifer was surprised to see how much time he spent teaching the boy.

"And," she adds, "one of the first things Stewart did when he was fired was buy a canoe and a kayak, and now they're off every weekend, just the two of them. I mean, he'd never done anything with Robert before. The boy is quite a loner, so he thinks it's just great to have his father as a friend and have something they are learning to do together. When they started, they got a roof rack for the car and learned how to stow a kayak and canoe on it. I thought they would be screaming at each other, which is what would have happened before, but it didn't this time, much to my amazement and delight."

A cynic might say it's all very well for parents to have fun with their kids while they are out of work, but what's going to happen when they get a new job? That cynic would have a good point. There's no telling what will happen when the pressures of work resume.

Janice is back at work, in a demanding, time-consuming job. She loves it, but is trying hard to balance the task of proving herself in a new organization with her need to make time for her children. "She feels guilty when she doesn't achieve that balance," Ross says, "but I know it helps a lot that I'm there with the kids. I think it's going to be a lot harder for her when I finish college and start work again. She hopes she'll have her job organized by then, so it won't require so many hours away from home, but I suspect she'll never be totally free of the guilt."

Stewart is now back at work, too. After a brief period of unemployment, he found an extremely good, exciting job. He's thoroughly enjoying it and he is continuing to enjoy his family. He still goes on those outings with Robert, and he recently went with Jennifer and their daughter on a tour of the colleges the girl is considering applying to. "That would never have happened before," Jennifer says. "Lindsey and I would've had to go by ourselves."

In many ways, the positive example of how a firing led to Stewart and his children becoming good friends is really just the converse of the negative stories of Gil and Ted and their kids. That is, over the course of a job search, the kids take their cues on how to behave from their parents. They may happily move right into the new order of things, as Jennifer and Stewart's children seem to be doing. They may be carrying on a guerilla balancing act, as Karen and Gil's two children are doing. But in each case they are responding to the strongest messages conveyed to them by their parents.

In a situation as emotionally charged as a dismissal and its aftermath, it's essential that parents find ways to reassure their children that they are all right and that everyone in the family will survive the crisis. Children of every age need this reassurance, and if they receive unmistakable cues to this effect, they will generally be all right themselves and behave accordingly.

By far the most effective assurance that everything is fine comes from parents who truly believe that they are all right.

Again we can offer few better examples than that offered by Molly and Fred. In their case, previous crises had given them a great store of emotional resources with which to meet Fred's firing, and reassuring their married daughters that they were all right was a fairly simple matter. "At the beginning, they were hurting for their dad," Molly says. "The whole tone of everything they said was 'Poor Daddy, how much more can the poor man take?' That sort of stuff. But once they saw that Fred was holding up, and that I was holding up, they stopped worrying. Now it's amazing how often they call and don't even ask, 'Has Dad found anything?' They'll be happy when he does, but they're not dwelling on it."

It's frequently difficult to attain, but that is pretty well the ideal attitude. Another ideal is when a termination crisis becomes a learning experience for children. We've already mentioned parents who view a firing as a way of preparing their children for the future and the new business realities. We also met several spouses of fired people who reported that their kids learned lessons that they could (and generally had to) apply right away.

For example, one man told us: "My teenage daughter got a part-time job so she could have extra spending money that we couldn't give her. She has learned how to apply for jobs and be responsible to her employer. She's very proud to be earning her own money and even refused to accept the weekly allowance we still wanted to give her."

Despite her own financial difficulties, another spouse seemed rather pleased that her children would, for a while, have to learn how to do without many of the resources and privileges that their dad's huge salary had always given them. "Okay, so we have only one car now," she said. "They'll just have to organize themselves accordingly."

Making allowances for the fact that her kids are considerably younger, Pat felt much the same way after she had decided to rise to the occasion of her husband's dismissal by returning to school and learning a practical skill.

"The kids were very good about it, even though there were some instances where I usually would have been there for them and I wasn't. But I think they coped well. There were times when they didn't want to cope, of course, but we told them they had to, that this is reality and they had to take some of the responsibility.

"We believe the kids are a real part of the household, so they have chores. Not excessive ones, but they are learning they have to pull their weight, too. I'm not saying it's always pleasant and they accept everything we say. Sometimes I had a test the next day, so I had no time to read their bedtime stories. That never went down well. Sometimes I felt terrible and very guilty about what I was doing. But you know, no one died and we chugged along, and in the long run, no harm's done. It was probably a growing experience for them. They're loved, they have a good home and Daddy did get a job he likes."

The Kids' Reactions to the Job Search

Considering the many domestic ups and downs that can result from Mom or Dad spending more time than usual at home, it is often easy to forget the central event: the job search. But that is not to say the kids are unaware of it. Indeed, some are keenly aware and often very interested, and they react to it in a variety of ways, some helpful, others not.

Interest in the Search

Where parents establish an atmosphere of open communication, children of all ages will tend to be interested and inquisitive. Jason and Gabriella have very young children, and their involvement is limited to asking "Have you got a job yet?" or "Are you going for an interview?" when they see their father going in and out of the house.

Theresa and Ray's two university-age sons are actually involved in discussions about which jobs he should apply for. This is nothing new. That family has always discussed its affairs and made decisions together.

More typical is the situation reported by Sheila, who said her sons were kept informed about which companies Desmond was applying to. Now and then they would ask how the search was going, and sometimes there would be a flurry of family fun and excitement, as when Desmond went for an interview at an airline, which raised the possibility of free travel for everyone.

Sharing the Highs and Lows

Sheila was talking about the up side of the job search, the very real excitement that comes with the prospect of a promising new job. The down side comes when glittering job prospects don't pan out and the hunt drags on. These lows are to be expected, and when they occur, family members can help one another and learn from them. Angela, for instance, told us this: "We have the inevitable ups and downs, but we know the children are watching us and are aware of our moods, so we try to talk to them a lot. I've told them that even when I cry, this, too, is part of life. We're trying to teach them that our highs and lows are not strange or unusual."

Such sharing is generally beneficial, but unrestrained empathy can get out of hand. At Leslie's house, for example, it became the custom for everyone to eat dinner at home on the night before Paul went to an interview. Normally this would be a splendid morale booster. But, Leslie says, "sometimes the anxiety the children felt for him would come through. And the next day, before he went for the interviews, they'd get kind of excited, and I'd warn them not to expect every one of these to materialize into a job offer, but that was tough for them to understand. Their view was 'He's gone for an interview and he's my dad and he's great and he's going to get it.' And then, when the jobs didn't come through, they didn't know how to react to him. They'd say, 'Gee,' or 'That's too bad,' and I think Paul interpreted that as sort of another step down in their estimation. So sometimes he was afraid to let them know another job hadn't panned out."

Annoyance

Your mate's demands for silence while he or she works and other disruptions of family routines are bound to annoy the kids. One of the biggest bones of contention is often the job seeker's appropriation of the telephone. One family solved the problem by installing the call-waiting feature. Thus their teenage daughter could use the phone pretty well whenever she wanted, but with the understanding that if a call came through for her dad, she had to get off the line immediately.

Difficulty Understanding the Search

We have just seen how the failure of Leslie's children to understand what a job search entails put additional pressure on their father. This is not a pervasive problem, but one to watch out for, because the pressure of a child's impatience with the length of the search, or the belief that Mom or Dad is being too choosy, could become a factor in the rash acceptance of an unsuitable job. The way to avoid such pressure is to impress upon your kids the importance of finding the right job and give them a realistic idea of the time it may take Mom or Dad to find it.

Jane told us that at one point she felt her boys were getting too impatient, and she tried to give them a lesson in the facts of job-search life: "I tried to explain that it took a while, and we were allowing a year, because Gavin didn't want to take just any job that was out there and that the higher your level, the fewer jobs there are."

Helpfulness

One of the strongest messages that spouses gave to us was that children can be very helpful during a job search. On the purely practical level, they can relieve some of the stress and tension at home by helping around the house, and they often prove to be indispensable message takers.

But above all, they can be a great source of distraction, fun and laughter, simply by being themselves and continuing to be engaged in their own activities. As one woman put it: "My thirteen-year-old is like a whirlwind. She is full of life and activity. It's just a joy to be in the same house with her."

Children, especially the older ones, can also be deliberately supportive and thoughtful. For example, Elaine's one source of solace was the support and emotional generosity that her daughter freely offered. "She was always saying, 'What would Daddy do without you? Keep it up, Mom. He needs you.'" Remember, Elaine was not confiding in anyone else, so this support meant a great deal to her.

In a lighter vein, Emily and Wayne's sons help to keep their morale up by remaining their thoughtful, cheerful selves. "They don't try to smother us with sympathy or anything like that," Emily says. "They call and ask, 'Anything yet, Dad?' And last week, Bob rang and said, 'Dad, do you want to come and work at our shop?' It was just a joke. Bob had just expanded his music store and was looking for extra clerks. So Wayne said, 'No, you've got the wrong guy. Call your brother.' He meant Victor, our youngest. He's just out of college and still looking for a job, so he and Wayne talk about job search techniques and swap leads."

Bob was joking there, but older children can be an important part of your partner's contact network. We must also note that Bob, who is married and has a family of his own, told Emily and Wayne that they could come and live with them if worse came to worst. Since Wayne had been out of work for more than a year, it was more than an idle gesture, and a comfort to the parents.

Bob's offer was typical of the way a considerable number of children were prepared to make significant sacrifices for their parents and the family. When she heard about her father's dismissal, Olive and Craig's daughter immediately offered to quit school and get a job. The offer was immediately rejected. But when Rosemary and Reg's sons volunteered to transfer from their private school to a public high school in order to save money, their offer was accepted. The reason for this was that the boys had realized that since Reg's dismissal meant family funds were short, their younger sister might never have a chance to go to a private school. They were in their last year and had already received most of what a private school can offer. Therefore, they reasoned, it was only fair that the money be used to ensure that their sister would have the same advantage.

We also heard of two boys who, realizing the great sacrifices their unemployed parents were making in order for them to continue the activities they loved, announced that they really didn't want to go camp the following summer.

The parents knew what the boys were doing and had to develop a counter-strategy to ensure that they did go without feeling bad about it. "I'll never forget what they did," their father said to us. "That gesture made me very proud of them."

Equally proud, and somewhat taken aback, were the unemployed parents of a young woman who was going to college the following autumn. Her tuition and other expenses were covered by scholarships, so she got a summer job and turned her earnings over to her mom and dad.

Not all kids are helpful, of course. But we found that many children, especially older ones with their own families, don't often help out for the simple reason that their parents are reluctant to let them know how they're feeling or what they need. To take just one example, in chapter two we noted that Carol Ann was afraid of having to move to her and Colin's remote vacation home. She also told us that she gets terribly frustrated when she mentions the matter to her married daughter, who always responds by saying how nice the move would be for her and Daddy. But what else could the daughter say? Carol Ann has never once hinted to her kids that she's terrified of being stuck out in the sticks, so how could her daughter be expected to respond with anything other than polite interest?

Which brings us back to Leslie. Earlier in this chapter we saw how her children's efforts to cheer on Paul's job search occasionally backfired and further demoralized him. But Leslie had another point to make in that connection: "That hypersupportive phase was really only at the beginning of the search. You know how kids are. As time went on, they began to go back into their own lives and sometimes you'd think they'd completely forgotten about Paul's situation. I don't know how many times they were up in the air about one of their own little problems and I had to say to them, 'You can't go to your father with things like that right now. Talk to me. Don't hit him the moment he comes through the door with I need the car and can I have this and I gotta have that.' Usually they were pretty good about it. They'd come to me, and we would channel the problem or whatever through to Paul at appropriate moments."

Many other spouses had similar stories. That is, over time, if the marital relationship is reasonably stable and life settles into its new patterns, most kids will become accustomed to the situation and, to use Pat's word, "chug" along with their lives in a relatively normal manner.

The payoff comes when the parent finally gets another job. As we have seen with Leslie and her children, the storms and crises (and periods of forgetfulness) that punctuated the job search suddenly give way to their joy in, and sharing of, Mom or Dad's triumph. There is, to be sure, an element of self-interest here, as we saw with Stephanie and Alan's daughters' concern about Christmas presents. But largely it is joy for its own sake and the concomitant sense of having paid for this moment with their own sacrifices, both material and emotional.

Thus, speaking of the slight deprivations her children endured during Mark's job search, Pat commented: "They were involved in the loss and they were involved in the gain. When Mark got that lovely new job, they were as excited and happy as we were, and they've been down to his office several times already. I don't think there are any lasting scars there." Which brings us to one last point. As resilient as children are, the firing and tensions of the job search are still not something they can easily forget.

Millie, for example, told us that months after Aaron had found a new job their young children were still asking, "Are you the boss, Daddy? Do you have a boss?" It was as if they had decided that if Daddy was the boss, no one would ever fire him again.

COPING

» 1. Tell the children about the dismissal as soon as possible, giving information appropriate to their ages. Keep them informed about the job search, also in appropriate detail.

» 2. Before you tell them anything, however, you and your partner should discuss what approach you will be taking to the firing and the reason for it that you will give to the children. Moreover, it is important that you inform them of the firing together. This will prevent the kids from being confused by two different points of view. It will also be helpful to have both parents available to answer questions and be alert to their concerns.

» 3. Similarly, both parents should discuss what changes will affect the children and how they will approach them with that information. The more united the parents are in relation to the children, the better.

» 4. Keep the lines of communication open so the children feel free to talk to you about their concerns. Ask them directly about how they are feeling. Pent-up, unexpressed emotions and fears can lead to depression, even in the very young. The key here is to listen carefully to what they say, so you can respond in an honest, reassuring manner. Being open with them is a model for them being open with you.

» 5.   Be alert to changes in your children's behavior that could signal they are having difficulty, and remember that their actions don't necessarily have to be problematic. Your child could be a little more clingy, quiet, or even more active or talkative than usual. The clues are often subtle. But if you detect any and take time to talk to your children and find out if anything might be worrying them, it could help dissipate fears that might otherwise escalate unnecessarily. Remember the girl who decided that her parents were contemplating divorce.

» 6.   Remember that children have a way of blaming themselves when things go wrong in a family. For example, we know of one teenager who found innumerable excuses to be away from home at dinner time, because she felt guilty about how much it cost her parents to feed her. If you detect any such signs, make it clear to your kids that neither the situation nor any of its consequences are their fault.

» 7.   If a child has a question for one parent, it's best if he or she can ask that parent directly, rather than having to go through the other one.

» 8.   Be clear about the reason for the firing that you will be giving to outsiders and make sure that the children understand it. Suggest what they should say publicly, if asked, and make sure they can repeat it correctly. Knowing that they will be able to respond appropriately to such questions will add to their (and your) comfort and may ease any embarrassment they might feel.

» 9.   If possible, tell the kids about other parents they may know who have been through the same thing. This will help them realize that such a crisis is not unique to their family and that people do survive it. They might also feel less alone if they talk to the children in those families.

» 10. Let your children's school know about your situation and request that the teachers, school nurse and counsellors be alert for any problems or changes.

» 11. With teenagers, it's often hard to tell if behavioral changes are a normal part of adolescence or direct reactions to the firing and the new regime at home. If there are any problems in your household, you can find many good books on adolescence at the public library; and maybe a chat with a counselor will help clear the air.

» 12. Don't hesitate to seek counseling assistance, to help your children deal with the termination crisis. You don't need to have a specific problem. You might just want some help in learning how to talk with each other.

» 13. Make it clear what the family can and cannot afford and give the children precise spending boundaries. This will help you avoid the fairly common situation in which parents become hurt and upset because the kids seem totally insensitive to the family's financial position. Often they simply haven't been told what that position is.

» 14. Assess your financial situation carefully. While most parents work hard to maintain their kids' standard of living, it is important to determine the practicality of doing this. Specifically, can you do it without suffering or sacrificing in other important areas of your lives, or without putting too much extra pressure on yourselves? If you create expectations of continuing normalcy, the kids will proceed as if that is the case. If things cannot go on the same, then you must prepare the children for the changes to come, explaining why these are necessary and how they will be affected by them. If you are frank and realistic, it will ease much of their anxiety and make them feel that they are key players in the family's overall response to the crisis.

» 15. In nonfinancial areas, as well, enlist your kids' support in whatever ways might be helpful to you. In other words, don't be afraid to ask for their help.

» 16. Let the children know if you're having a rough day. They'll probably sense it anyway, so you needn't go into a lot of detail. Just a comment or two will (*a*) perhaps make you feel better, (*b*) tell the kids that your mood isn't their fault, (*c*) send them a clear signal that today isn't the day to pester you and (*d*) allow them to be supportive.

» 17. Make decisions as a couple about the kids. If there is a problem, sit down as husband and wife and try to find the solution you can both live with.

» 18. Stress is a normal reaction to change, but you can help give your children the extra security they need at this time by keeping the family schedule as close to normal as possible.

» 19. If you have someone who helps you with the children or the household, discuss the situation with that person and decide how you can best maintain everyone's routines.

» 20. If a move becomes a very real possibility, let the children know about it as soon as possible and promise to tell them the moment you have definite information. If the move does become necessary, there are many ways you can help them adjust positively to the change. One of these is just being available to discuss their concerns. Also, in the list of books that we provide at the end, you will find details on how to obtain an excellent booklet called *Kids on the Move*, which explains how children of different ages feel about moving and has many wonderful suggestions on how parents can help them cope with the situation.

» 21. Above all, be aware of the importance of time in children's adjustments to change.

Chapter Seven

The Two of You and Your Extended Family

A couple's parents, brothers, sisters, aunts, uncles, cousins and in-laws can have a significant impact on their capacity to cope with a termination. These are the people we naturally turn to for emotional support and comfort in times of crisis, and in most cases they will provide it without question. But a firing means different things to different people, and the family can respond to a dismissal in ways that may leave you and your partner feeling hurt and confused. We are by no means saying you should expect the worst from your extended family, but neither should you be surprised if their response to your partner's job loss is not always what you'd like it to be. To take the edge off any surprises your family might have in store for you, we offer the following. It is a distillation of what the spouses of people who had lost their jobs told us about their families' reactions to the firing and its aftermath, and we hope you will discover in their experiences something of value for yourself.

The Family May Indeed Offer Support

Well over half the spouses said their families were supportive from the moment they got the news. And when parents and other family members did respond to the dismissal with genuine empathy and understanding, the couples tended to be relieved and grateful. This was because job loss is often followed by feelings of shame and embarrassment, and knowing that the people they most cared about were not going to withdraw their love and respect was enormously reassuring.

Murray provided this glowing illustration of our point: "Adele's mom was flabbergasted by the firing. She thinks her daughter can do anything and couldn't imagine how the company could let her go. She went on and on about Adele's skills and abilities, which was just great for Adele's ego. Her mother lives in Rochester, and I swear, the very next day she got on a plane to come and be with her daughter. For a full week, she cooked for us and took Adele shopping and generally helped to distract her from the dismissal. I can't tell you how much we both really appreciated her visit and her kindness."

In the same vein, Molly told us how thankful Fred was to receive a friendly call from her father and how much he appreciates occasional calls from his out-of-town brother. These are not heavy, my-heart-is-bleeding-for-you responses to the firing. They are affable, open chats about a number of things, laced with appropriate expressions of concern for Fred and interest in his job search.

Usually that's all that is needed in the way of family support. Thus when Angela's mother stopped buying products made by Percy's former employer, her gesture was greatly appreciated but not necessary. Where she and other members of the family really came through was in the thoughtful way they showed their concern directly. That is, they didn't overwhelm the couple with phone calls, and when they did call, they didn't pester them with questions about how Percy's job search was going. Instead they asked how Percy and Angela were managing and left it up to them to impart as much information as they wanted. They behaved like old friends, rather than self-appointed job-search monitors who were calling to check up on the couple.

Family members can also be a superb source of advice, based on their experience of the world in general and their specific knowledge of the couple. Relatives who've been through a dismissal themselves may be a particular comfort. Mary Ellen, for example, spoke of how Derek's firing deepened his relationship with his father. "Derek's basically a loner, but his family means a lot to him," she said. "His father is a great person, and at one point he had been through something similar, though I don't think they talked about it very much at the time. But right after Derek was let go, we went over to his parents' place to tell them the news. All the way there, he couldn't stop talking about the problems the dismissal would bring, which meant he was really worried. When we told them, his mom and dad were shocked but very caring, and his dad took him out to the garden, where the two of them could talk privately. Every now and then I'd look out the window and see them there, sitting side by side, just quietly talking. They were like that for an hour and a half, and when they came in, Derek looked so much better. For a while we went to his parents' place every second night. We shared our worries with them, and they helped us to think a lot of things through. Derek spent many hours with his father, and they became closer than ever. His father helped him very much. He never tore him down, only built him up, and I think that was extremely important for Derek."

Similarly, you or your partner may find a special confidante among your pool of relatives, if you don't have one already. Irene did this. Her husband, Kevin, told us about how, after a month of listening to her go on and on about the injustice of her dismissal, he didn't want to hear any more. "Irene was upset that I was sick of hearing about 'the unfairness of it all,' " Kevin said. "But when I backed out of these sessions, she turned to her sister, who at that point had far more patience and sympathy than I did."

The Absence of Family Support

This comes about for three basic reasons: First, a couple may not have any family or the family is geographically so distant that beyond an occasional telephone call they are virtually out of reach. This can be very difficult and isolating for a couple, especially those who would be most comfortable talking to family and really have no one else they trust in the same way. One man described the situation like this: "Both our parents died several years ago. My wife lost her job last summer and went through some very bitter negotiations with the company. It was a tough time for us, and we felt really alone. In periods like that, you need people around you who know you at the most basic level and, sometimes just by being there, can remind you that you're more than your job."

The second reason for a lack of family support is that the couple doesn't tell the family about the firing, either out of embarrassment or a desire not to worry them. Whatever the reason, keeping the family in the dark usually closes an important avenue of support, and leaves the couple vulnerable to an embarrassing revelation of their deception. Such was the case when Mary Beth's brother phoned Martin's former company and was told he hadn't been there for weeks. The couple then had to not only explain why they had withheld the news, but also try to re-establish the previous level of trust that they and their families had enjoyed.

The third reason family support may be lacking is that the firing is overshadowed by other life events, such as family illness, deaths and problems with children.

Worry About Parents

Often in cases where couples didn't want to burden aged or ailing parents with news of the termination, they still told the rest of the family, then took one of two courses.

When parents were far away and had little chance of learning about the dismissal, some people decided to withhold the news, figuring there was little chance of discovery. However, when Emily did this, she quickly learned that it's not always so easy. With her parents in Wales, her father was told, but her mother, who had suffered a stroke, was not. But the mother is still pretty sharp, and she soon sensed that something was not quite right with Emily and Wayne. So now, whenever Emily talks to her on the phone or replies to one of her letters, she has to be exceptionally creative in answering her mother's questions truthfully, but without spilling the beans.

Other couples took the less risky, more solid course of preparing themselves carefully and then telling their folks about the firing. This largely meant waiting a few days until they had composed themselves and learned the details of their financial situation. Thus they could approach their parents calmly and provide them with realistic assurance that they would be okay during the job search. Molly and Fred were especially concerned about her seventy-six-year-old parents, because these people had in the past worried a great deal about Fred's alcoholism. Therefore Molly and Fred sorted out their finances and then drove to the city where her parents lived to tell them in person. As is often the result when parents are given realistic assurances, Molly's folks became very supportive and reassuring.

Of course, everyone must evaluate his or her own family circumstances, but most parents are a lot tougher than their children give them credit for, and the kids can end up protecting people who do not need protection.

Before you decide to tell or not tell your parents about the dismissal, ask yourselves these two crucial questions: What is the worst thing that can happen if we do tell them? If that did happen, how could we handle it?

Family Can Provide Concrete Support

We found many instances of this, and here are only a few examples. Maggie's mother helped her look after the kids, which made this stressful period much more bearable and gave Maggie and Doug some much-needed time alone. Murray's parents made it clear that financial support was available at any time. Adele's severance pay was substantial, and the couple didn't need the money, but when Adele had the odd panicky moment, it was reassuring for her to know that emergency funding was only a phone call away. Linda's sister twice allowed her to use her cottage to get away with the kids for ten days of fun and respite from the stresses at home. Leslie's aunt kept an eye open for appropriate job ads and clipped them out of the paper and passed them on to Paul. And Angela's sister loaned her and Percy a car to replace the company vehicle that had been taken away from him and left the family all but stranded in the suburbs. The need for a car can be extremely stressful for a couple if they do not have the funds or do not want to use their severance pay to buy one because they don't know how much money will be required to get them through the job search. Thus Angela's sister provided not only deeply appreciated concrete assistance, but also a timely lift to the couple's spirits.

In addition to assistance of the kind just noted, family members can also make concrete contributions to the job search. When we were talking to Maria, for example, she told us that Howard's hottest job prospect emanated from a tip by his sister, who works in the same industry. And back in chapter one we told you about Theresa's husband, Ray, who got a job after meeting a company president at a party at his sister-in-law's cottage. Ray had not been backward about telling his family that he needed help, and his sister-in-law had no reservations about introducing him to this executive. As it happened, the man did not have a specific opening at the time, but he saw Ray's potential for solving organizational problems and within four days had created an appropriate position and hired him.

Family Members May Appear Indifferent

An apparent lack of interest or concern by family members can reflect a number of things. One of these may be a feeling of awkwardness or embarrassment about termination. This generally comes from older people who still view a firing as a stigma. Thus they may assume that the issue also makes you uncomfortable and refrain from mentioning the subject because of their own discomfort and misplaced concern for your feelings. It would be difficult to exaggerate how powerful this motive is. For example, during the fourteen months he was out of work, Ray's mother never once mentioned it. When he got his new job, she invited him and Theresa over for breakfast, saying, "It's so nice to be able to talk to you again."

A significant contemporary wrinkle on this way of thinking was reported by Ross and Janice. Back in chapter three, we saw how Janice's family refused to understand the type of work she was looking for and badgered her to take the job in the glove shop. Ross and Janice believe her family's indifference to her talents and ambition came in large part from what Ross called "a stereotyped view of men's and women's roles. I honestly think they saw me as the sole breadwinner because I'm male, and they gave no credence at all to Janice's job, even though she'd been making more money than me. They thought of her job as unnecessary, a source of what used to be called pin money." Like Janice's family, some people still don't take women's jobs as seriously as they do men's, and as a result, women often receive less sympathy when they lose their jobs.

Other reasons for the family's apparent indifference could be that they have total faith in your partner's ability to get another job. Or maybe they do not understand how hard a termination can hit a couple. And there is always this to consider: perhaps you are consciously or unconsciously telling them by your manner that you do not wish to talk about the termination.

Family Disapproval

In certain cases, family members will be far from indifferent to the firing. No matter how the couple behaves, they'll be openly hostile, and to illustrate this hurtful and disruptive phenomenon, we have two compelling examples.

The first involves Elaine, whose father was a stern, extremely wealthy, status-conscious man. To his mind, Elaine always seemed out of step, and she never won anything resembling acceptance or approval from her family until she and James had achieved a level of financial success that was consistent with her father's values. Then James was fired. This was early in their marriage. He and Elaine were living away from their hometown at the time, and when she phoned her father and said she and James were coming home, he bellowed, "Don't you have any pride? How can you come back here when your husband is such a failure?" Elaine was out of step again. Nevertheless she and her husband went home and, over the years, endured an endless succession of slights from her family. As a result, when James suffered his second firing and Elaine was faced with the enormous tasks of trying to help him out of his depression and coping with the prospect of immediate bankruptcy, she could not bring herself to ask for her family's help and support. As tough and as painful as it was, it was still easier for her to keep quiet about her misfortune and try to survive on her own.

The second example is much less extreme, but for that reason, we are sorry to say, all the more common than Elaine's situation. It concerns Gabriella's mother, who has a profound, old-fashioned disapproval of being fired. She lives in Scotland, and in normal circumstances, Gabriella would not have told her about Jason's firing because she just didn't need the extra grief. However, her mother happened to be visiting when Jason was terminated, so she had to be told, and her presence severely limited the couple's efforts to come to terms with the event. Even when they tried to discuss the matter privately, they could still feel her mother's disdainful presence, which constrained the flow and ease of their conversation.

For both Elaine's father and Gabriella's mother, the imagined stigma of the firing itself was the primary source of disapproval. With Gabriella's mother, and the parents of many other spouses we met, there was also concern for the son or daughter's welfare and a sense that the sons- or daughters-in-law had let their mates and them down. Such attitudes are bound to be extremely painful and disappointing to a couple.

Yet, given the strength of the emotional bonds that often exist between family members, it may be very difficult for the couple to get their parents and other relatives to change their attitudes when these people actually voice their disapproval.

An example of how difficult and complex this can be comes from Ross. Earlier we saw how his parents not only seemed to think his job loss was his fault, they told people he was still employed. As noted, their behavior might have stemmed from fear or embarrassment for their son. But it should not be forgotten that Ross was using the opportunity offered by his dismissal to go back to school and rethink his career goals—something that people who'd learned the rules of life and work during the Depression would find difficult, if not impossible, to understand.

Finally, if the relationship between either or both partners and members of their families were strained before the dismissal, family disapproval is bound to add to the strain. Another thing to be aware of is when family members have something critical to say, they usually pick the spouse to say it to. That is, the sensitivity that restrains them from speaking their minds to the job seeker seems to disappear when it comes to being open with his or her spouse.

Such attitudes may contribute to job seekers' already diminished self-esteem and fan the doubts their spouses may secretly harbor about their mates' responsibility for the firing and the effectiveness of their job searches. This can seriously undermine the spouses' capacity to be supportive and may impose a debilitating strain on their marital relationships.

Other scenarios resulting from family disapproval include spouses trying to placate their own family members and, in turn, defending them to a partner who is resentful of their attitudes. Or, if a woman, say, tells her husband that she doesn't like the way her in-laws are badmouthing him, she may be surprised to find that he does not appreciate her criticism of his parents. In short, navigating the turbulent waters of family loyalties is difficult at the best of times. After a termination, it can be a painful and risky endeavor.

Family Pressure on the Job Search

We began this book by noting that in our parents' day jobs were generally lifetime things and a firing was a disgraceful rarity. Consequently, when one of their children is fired, parents worry beyond reason. As a result, rather than being a source of support for the couple that is facing the termination, it is the parents who need the most help, and the couple have to expend their energy being reassuring at a time when in fact they need to be reassured.

Furthermore, in a close variation of this scenario, when parents and other well-meaning family members are not content to worry, they act. That is, unlike Angela and Percy, who received thoughtful, well-timed calls from her family, some couples are beset by frequent calls from relatives whose persistent concern makes them feel as if they have to explain why a job hasn't materialized in the past two days. Generally, these callers are unaware of the needless pressure to which they are subjecting the couple. However, we have also come across situations where equally well-meaning relatives deliberately apply pressure to a couple, often via the spouse. For example, back in the marriage chapter we saw how, while Leslie was still reeling from the shock of Paul's dismissal, his family was pestering her to get on his back and hustle him out into the job market.

Such callers are not being intentionally insensitive. Most often they are truly concerned about the couple's well-being, or they are driven by fears resulting from other dismissals or tough times their families have experienced. It never occurs to them that they are only adding to the couple's tensions and distress and that the basic good-heartedness behind their calls is not much solace to the victims of their uncontrolled concern.

About the only countermeasure available to you is the risky business of politely informing such people that their concern is something of an overreaction. Clearly explain your job search plan to them and assure them that you and your partner have a financial plan in place. If you are calm and firm, it will do a lot to provide them with the reassurance they need. If, despite all your efforts, they still keep on calling every other day, you might consider using an answering machine to intercept them. You'll still have to call them back, but you can do so at a time of your own choosing.

Family Can Provide Perspective

In heartening contrast to relatives who apply pressure to a couple are family members who can ease stress by putting things into a positive perspective.

Derek's parents, whom we mentioned earlier in this chapter, are a marvelous case in point. Not only did they take the time to help Derek and Mary Ellen think through their anxieties, they also led by example. Having been through a dismissal themselves, they were living proof of how well a couple can survive a firing.

Sue Ann's family does much the same, offering the wisdom of their own life experiences and frequently reminding her and Buck, "You're not sick, you have your health and you have each other. You're both bright, capable people. There's really nothing to worry about."

In Angie's case there really are things to worry about, particularly her continual distress over the direction of Greg's job search. However, she does listen to, and take some comfort from, her mother's gentle concern and her different way of looking at the situation. As Angie puts it, "When I'm feeling down and I talk to my mother, I can tell she understands me. But she also reminds me that Greg was very unhappy in his last job and asks if I want to go through that aggravation again. When she says that, I have no choice. I have to agree with her that maybe his release was all for the best."

In a similar vein, before his termination, Maggie's husband, Doug, was excessively devoted to his job and neglecting his family. Maggie's mother talked to him about it, saying, "Doug, this is no life." He didn't change immediately, but he has now started to address the imbalances in his life, and his mother-in-law's carefully chosen remarks could very well have marked the point where he began to see his wife and children and his relationships with them differently.

We are talking about perspective here, not overnight remedies. But the wisdom of parents and other respected and trusted family members, plus the alternative viewpoints they may bring to the situation, can have an immeasurable effect on the smoothness and duration of the couple's passage through Limbo.

COPING

» 1. Remember, in most cases there is nothing to be gained (and lots to be lost) by keeping news of your partner's termination from the family.

» 2. You can minimize parents' and other family members' worry by telling them about the firing in a reassuring, optimistic and realistic manner. It is generally wise to have your financial plans in place before you talk to them. This will lend authority to your reassurance, and you may even wish to share some of the details with them. You won't be doing your relatives or yourselves any good if you engage in protracted worrying sessions with them. Instead, try to educate them about today's job market, the importance of finding the right position and the time and other factors involved in a job search in your partner's industry and at his or her level.

» 3. Similarly, it makes a great deal of sense for you and your partner to discuss his or her skills and job targets with your respective families. This is also a good time to ask them to let you know if they have any contacts, job leads or suggestions.

» 4. If family members are negative or disapproving, find a way to put a stop to it. One way is to tell them that even though they may think such thoughts, nothing will be gained by expressing them to you and your partner. Then change the subject to more interesting and pleasant topics.

» 5. Finally, if you need to take the bull by the horns and tell your family that you don't appreciate a constant barrage of questions, be very diplomatic. One tactic here is to explain that you and your partner try to cope with the pressures and uncertainty of the job search by doing your best to forget about it from time to time and their calls often come just when you have managed to forget about it briefly and are enjoying a momentary return to normal family life. Assure them that you'll let them know if you have any significant news—and be sure you do that.

Chapter Eight

The Two of You and Your Friends

Along with family, friends are the people a couple looks to for support in times of crisis, and usually they provide it. However, after a firing there are almost always some surprises. This is particularly true in the case of friendships with former colleagues and their spouses. The termination removes the individual from everyday contact with that community, and it is at this point that, as more than one spouse told us, "You certainly find out who your friends are!" On the whole, though, with some unpleasant exceptions, a couple's friends do rally round after a termination.

Finding Others Who've Been Fired, Too

When people's partners are fired and they begin to tell others about it, they frequently discover that many of their acquaintances have already been through a dismissal. This tends to be reassuring and affirming, because it tells them that their partners are not unusual and that other people have survived the experience and gone on to do other things. Moreover, these people are often excellent sources of firsthand advice.

Telling Friends

Some couples did it immediately, and their friends were an important source of comfort and affirmation, showing them that they were not alone and allowing them to deal aloud with the shock and grief of the dismissal. Other couples felt they had to have some time alone before telling their friends.

As we have demonstrated, some misguided couples didn't tell anyone. This was especially hard on the spouses who did not themselves wish to keep the firing a secret, but whose partners insisted on a policy of silence. They understood the embarrassment and other feelings that lay behind their mates' need for privacy and felt they should respect their wishes. But at the same time they sorely needed the comfort and assurance that their partners were generally too hurt, preoccupied or worried to provide, and they became frustrated and angry at the way they had been shut off from their support networks.

One such spouse couldn't take it any more and decided to take action. She swore her best friend to secrecy and told her what she had been going through. However, the relief that this brought was quickly obliterated by an inescapable feeling that she had betrayed her husband. She remained in that no-win situation until she finally had a heart-to-heart talk with her husband and convinced him that their secrecy was doing more harm than good.

Friends Take Their Cue From You

People who were open about the dismissal seemed to have friends who were willing to talk about it and discuss the job search at length. More private or reticent people generally found that their friends were hesitant to raise the subject beyond a casual inquiry about how things were going. One spouse, Frances, actually took charge of guiding her friends' behavior. She told them about the firing right away and said, "Please don't ask me about it. I'll let you know when I have some news." Her friends respected this, which enabled her to avoid talking about job prospects that might not pan out and allowed her to be with these people without having to talk about her and her husband's situation unless she wanted to. In short, she taught her friends how to be with her through the crisis in the way that would be most helpful to her.

The Invisible Partner

While friends are on the whole enormously supportive, their attention tends to focus on the fired partner. Few people seem to realize the impact of a firing on the spouse and how difficult the experience is for him or her. At any rate, the spouses we talked to were seldom asked how they were feeling or coping with the job loss. This is largely a sin of omission, rather than commission. People don't deliberately withhold their concern. It's just that the fired partner is the obvious victim, while his or her spouse's wounds are so much more obscure.

Role Models

Several spouses told us that in the past they had observed friends whose partners were going through a termination crisis. Even if they did not discuss the situation at the time, they noted how their friends behaved. Then, when their own partners were fired, they recalled their friends' behavior and decided upon those attitudes and actions they wished to emulate and those they did not wish to repeat.

Confidantes

Most spouses told us how important it was to have at least one trustworthy friend with whom they could worry out loud and vent feelings that they feared would be hurtful or a burden to their partners. Elaine has told us how lonely and debilitating it was to have no such person. Stephanie, on the other hand, had a couple of close friends.

"There were days when there were tears and I was in a panic," she says. "I know I'm contradicting myself, but I really was in control. I was the backbone of our family, and I was always up for my husband. But sometimes I got tired of that, and when I was with a good friend, my emotions just pour-ed out. That was the hardest part of the whole ex-perience, always being up for Alan, so I truly needed those friends. You can never thank them enough for just being there."

Gabriella was equally fortunate. "Having my best friend to talk to was really a godsend," she told us. "There were times when I just needed to complain—complain about the way Jason was fired, complain about Jason, complain about all of it. And I knew Pam knew I really loved Jason and in a few hours or a day or two I wouldn't be so miserable and frustrated. So it was really great to know I could just let all my bad feelings spill out one day and be fine the next, without having someone say, 'Hey, only yesterday you were saying Jason's impossible, so how come he's an angel today?' Pam never ever judged me or what I said in any way."

In having Pam to talk to, Gabriella was also fortunate in that this woman had lived through her own husband's firing and an extended job search two years previously. Thus, although Pam might have been nonjudgmental in any circumstances, she listened and spoke with an informed empathy, which gave Gabriella complete freedom to say virtually anything she had to get off her chest.

Bob was equally lucky in having a close friend with whom he could talk about his concerns during Estelle's job search, though he assured us that his complaints were relatively few. However, it is not the number of grievances that are at issue here, it's the importance of having someone other than your partner with whom you can air your feelings.

Probably because it's not his style, Kevin had no one with whom he could vent his frustrations arising from Irene's disruptive presence at home. His only outlets were arguments with his wife and doubling the distance he ran every day.

In other words, a true confidante is indeed a godsend.

Supportive Friends and Acquaintances

Not all of your friends, of course, can be called confidantes in the truest sense of the word, but they can still be a tremendously stabilizing force in your life at this time. That is, continuing to see friends and to entertain and be entertained by them during a termination crisis provides a reassuring sense of normalcy. This is especially important to spouses whose partners are too preoccupied with their own worries to offer much companionship to their mates. Linda, for instance, refused to stop her life while Ben was lost in his efforts to start his business or, when that didn't work out, he moped around for eight months before starting his job search. Instead, when time allowed, Linda kept herself busy and active with her friends, doing a host of things, which ranged from searching for cheap but great ethnic restaurants to volunteering in an election campaign.

The great thing about real friends is they will always be there for you, even if you aren't feeling particularly social. For example, after Mark was fired, Pat needed some time by herself to think about the situation. Her friends continued to call her, and although, over the next few months, she declined their invitations to get together, she explained how she was feeling, asked for their understanding and told them how happy she was to know that they cared and were still there.

In some cases, couples were surprised to receive calls and offers of help from distant acquaintances, who proved to be friends they really didn't know they had. For example, despite her family's fierce disapproval, Elaine and James returned to their hometown. Shortly after they arrived, someone they knew only slightly sent flowers and then dropped by to personally welcome them back. This simple gesture went a long way to soften the couple's painful homecoming.

Somewhat similarly, Bob was especially grateful for the close friends he and Estelle continued to enjoy. "They distracted us from our worries, and there was no way they'd allow even a moment of self-pity," he said.

For their part, Ian and Carl were deeply appreciative of the interest their business associates demonstrated by asking about their wives' job searches. The queries were always casual, spur-of-the-moment things, but they were clearly expressions of care and concern for the couple.

So far we've mentioned only moral support, but virtually every spouse with whom we spoke told us about at least one thoughtful offer of concrete help by both acquaintances and close friends. These ranged from baby-sitting to theater tickets. Victoria received substantial discounts on clothes she needed for interviews from a friend who managed a high-end clothing store. And long after the event Stephanie still fondly remembered the night the lawyer who had reviewed

Alan's severance package took them out to dinner. Other friends gave them a car. It was just an old clunker, which the friends were about to sell for scrap, but it was exactly what Stephanie and Alan needed to tide them over until they decided how to replace his company car.

Friends, acquaintances and business associates were also a great source of job market information, contacts and leads. Theresa, for example, warmly related how two of Ray's former business associates often called and took him to lunch for the specific purpose of keeping him up to date on industry trends and news. As well as helping to maintain his morale, these lunches and the information he got from them enabled him to keep his job search focused on firms that were planning to expand and therefore had a high hiring potential.

Kevin's bridge partner arranged for Irene to meet with someone in his firm who needed help on a new project. As a result, Irene was given a short-term contract, which did much to rebuild her self-esteem and ease the strains on her marriage caused by her efforts to run Kevin's business and the household in general.

Another couple we know of were unwittingly instrumental in helping a friend get a job. After the husband was fired, they decided they could not afford to pay a contractor to do some planned alterations to their house, so they put the job on hold. However, when a friend who had been looking for work in their city told them he'd given up and was going home, they offered the job to him. He accepted it, and the work kept him in town for another four weeks. Near the end of that time he suddenly got a job offer from a company he had applied to months earlier.

That is a spectacular example of the simple truth that even the smallest thoughtful gesture can have the most profound effects.

Friends and Colleagues from Your Partner's Former Company

In most cases, when someone is fired, it also means he or she is being rudely ejected from day-to-day contact with his or her "second family," some of whom are very good friends. The question is, will these friends and their spouses remain friends with the fired person and his or her spouse? In Harriet's case, her colleagues did stay in touch and when she found a new job, she immediately recruited one of them, because they had made a great team.

In our work, we have encountered a few instances where people who have been dismissed got absolutely no calls from their former colleagues, and even if the fired person's relationships with his or her former colleagues had not been close, it was still extremely hurtful for the couple to feel that no one cared enough even to acknowledge what had happened. On the other side of that coin, we have also encountered a few instances where former colleagues and their spouses made an effort to remain friends with a couple and the couple quickly grew bored with these people because all they could talk about was the company that they no longer had in common.

Usually, though, a couple will find that some people will remain friends, while others drift away. If relationships with people in the latter category really matter, the loss of contact and subsequent sense of rejection can be very painful. This is especially so in small, one-company towns, where a couple's entire social life may involve only company people. The same can happen in large cities if a couple's social activities largely revolved around the job that was lost. Carol Ann and Colin are a vivid case in point. Their friendships with his colleagues and their spouses go back more than two decades, to the time they all came over from Belgium to set up the pipe plant. Although everyone in this "family" was extremely upset when Colin was fired, and although he and Carol Ann continue to see these people socially, the very bond that brought them together now no longer exists. Moreover, one of his closest friends got promoted to a variation of his old job. He heroically stifled his feelings and congratulated the fellow, but no one can pretend that their friendship will ever be the same. It's no exaggeration to say that in the long run, Carol Ann and Colin will have to recreate their social universe.

Loss of Other Friends

Occasionally friends who have nothing to do with your partner's former job will mysteriously stop calling and drift away. Perhaps they have a lot of old-fashioned ideas about firing and are embarrassed for you. Maybe they think termination is a contagious disease. Or perhaps there is something in your manner, or that of your partner, which suggests you no longer want to be bothered with anyone. Whatever the reason, being let down in this way by people you once considered friends is painful. However, more than a few spouses told us that as painful as it was at the time, learning who their true friends are, in the long run, was beneficial.

Self-Imposed Isolation from Friends

The most egregious example of this comes when a couple doesn't tell their friends about the job loss. The strain of remembering what they said to whom and otherwise maintaining the charade wears them out and they simply stop seeing people. This confuses their friends, who either back away themselves, or demand an explanation for this strange behavior. If the latter happens, the couple then has to decide whether to continue the lie or explain it, and it's hard to do either without feeling foolish.

Another, rather unique, form of isolation is experienced by homemakers whose husbands' daytime presence at home prevents them from maintaining previous levels of contact with their friends. Most often this is because the job search means that during business hours the telephone is his and his alone. And even if they do have time to call a friend, many women feel uncomfortable having their husbands within earshot of their conversations. In the same vein, having friends to the home during the day can be awkward, as most homemakers in this position are concerned about disturbing their husbands while they are working on their job searches.

Unhelpful, Insensitive or Hurtful Friends

Several spouses reported that friends wouldn't invite them along on outings they thought would be too expensive. Their "kindness" was received with mixed feelings. As one spouse, Josh, explained it to us, he appreciated their friends' intentions, but his wife's job loss had not left them destitute. Moreover, he said, "If we can't afford to do something we'll have no problem telling people about it, so we'd really appreciate having the decisions on what we can or cannot do left to us."

For her part, Linda was invited along on her and her friends' annual theater-and-shopping expedition to New York. "It wasn't my intention to spend a lot of money on clothes," she says. "If I'd seen something I liked, I could've bought it, but I think the fact that Ben was out of work was difficult for one of the girls to handle. She must've thought I was already reduced to wearing rags, because at one point she said she would never wear a skirt like the one I was wearing. Actually, it was one of my favorite skirts. I had a certain amount of money to spend, and the fact that I didn't have more wasn't bothering me. I could do all the basic things, like pay for my theater tickets and my share of our dinners, and I was happy just window shopping and chatting with the girls, but she had to keep needling me all the time we were there. I don't know what her problem was."

It's also worth noting that in some cases snapping of this sort only emerges after a job search has gone on for a considerable time. Carol Ann, for example, reported that as Colin's search dragged on, a few of her friends became incredibly insensitive in their remarks. "'Hasn't he got a job yet?' they would ask in a blaming tone of voice, and one even had the nerve to suggest that he couldn't be trying very hard." You can be sure Carol Ann did some hard thinking about these so-called friendships.

However, such incidents must not blind us to the fact that sometimes friends may react to a long job search in ways that only appear to be insensitive. That is, they may stop asking how things are going out of a well-meaning desire to avoid putting pressure on you by raising what they assume is a touchy issue. As Carol Ann and many other spouses and their partners discovered, people who are truly close friends will continue to be caring and sensitive.

Your Impact on Your Friends

So far we have largely dealt with your friends' reaction to the termination as something that happens to you and your partner. But the converse can be true, as well. Although they may not show it, what is happening to you could be having a profound impact on them. In fact, some friends may identify with your situation so strongly that they are afraid for their own economic security. Others may even envy you. This can happen when people who are trapped in stressful or unsatisfying jobs see a friend's job loss as a chance for him or her to find more appropriate work, or for the affected couple to start their own business. In the case of an older couple, their friends may be jealous if the firing has given them the option of early retirement. In other words, these people can see quite clearly that at the heart of a dismissal crisis there is an opportunity they wouldn't mind having themselves. We completely agree with this point of view, and in the next chapter we will look at what a number of couples ultimately made of their opportunities.

COPING

» 1. Tell your friends, social contacts and business associates the truth about the dismissal. You and your partner can discuss the wording in advance, but whatever you decide, state it clearly and simply and be sure to mention the reason for the dismissal and your belief that while this is indeed a time of uncertainty, it is also a chance to develop some new and interesting options for the future. As in your discussions with family members, it is also wise to add that you intend to allow whatever time is needed for your partner to find the right job.

» 2. Think about your needs and let your friends know how they can be most helpful to you and your partner. Friends are eager to help, but they often don't know how and will appreciate your directness and guidance.

» 3. This is a time to be with the people you most trust, so give some thought to with whom you want to spend your time. In short, be selective about your social time.

» 4. Don't waste your time worrying or fretting about friends who disappoint you. Focus instead on enjoying the support and caring of those who do come through. Nurture those relationships as much as you can and chalk the others up to experience.

» 5. Sympathy wears out quickly, so look for an empathetic person you can talk to, be it a good friend, a doctor, a member of the clergy or a counselor. There is no better coping aid than a third party who has no stake in the matter and who won't hold the things you want to get off your chest against you.

» 6. It's helpful to talk to others who have been, or are going through, the same experience. Swapping stories, concerns, suggestions and advice is an extremely invigorating tonic.

» 7. Be careful not to isolate yourself from your friends. Making time for your social relationships, fun and relaxation is a pleasant and very helpful way of keeping your troubles in perspective.

» 8. If some of your friends stop calling, don't just retreat into an assumption that they are avoiding you. Give them a call. There could be any number of reasons why they haven't called that have nothing to do with you.

» 9. Finally, a small but irritating problem that some spouses wonder how to handle: neighbors who are curious about why your partner is suddenly home for a large part of the day. Take a tip from Gabriella. The neighbors she considered to be her friends were told immediately about Jason's dismissal. As for the others, if they asked, she told them, too, and if they didn't ask, she didn't tell them. Simple.

Chapter Nine

Recovery

Believe us, although it often seems as if it's never going to, your partner's job search eventually will be resolved. After all those long months of unreturned phone calls, false leads, dashed hopes and fruitless interviews, he or she will find a new opportunity. It is only natural that you will then assume that life can return to normal, that most of your money worries are over and that you and your family are free to start planning for the future.

However, once a new job has been found or a new business is under way, it is important to be prepared for the many new adjustments that will be required of every member of the family. These include debt repayment, possibly tighter budgets, new routines to which everyone will have to adapt, new information to absorb (including the names of your partner's new colleagues, the nature of the job and the company's culture and practices), and, probably to your surprise, new emotional needs to be addressed.

In our experience, the changes demanded by what lies ahead coexist with the changes brought about by the past. Most spouses, their partners and their children discover they need time to gain perspective on the job loss experience. Therefore, before getting to the ways in which families are indeed recovering well, we must first look at the way spouses deal with the emotional residue left by the termination crisis.

In most cases, the biggest emotional burden that spouses have to contend with after the crisis is over is their belief that it's somehow wrong or unnatural to feel the way they do, when in fact it would be unnatural not to retain some lingering traces of the hurt and other emotions they dealt with during the crisis.

The key thing to be aware of is that after a dismissal and the subsequent period of unemployment, life is never quite the same. For one thing, many spouses never regain the sense of security and confidence in the system that they enjoyed before the axe fell. They remain ill at ease, worrying and speculating that it will fall again.

Sheila likened the feeling to the uneasiness that haunts people who have survived a house fire. And Leslie had this to say: "Paul's very happy in his new job, but there's a lot of tension on my part, because his brother got a new job and was very happy in that and got fired six months later. So it's like waiting for the other shoe to drop. Six months and two days from now, maybe I'll be a bit more relaxed, but not right now.

"I know I shouldn't, but when Paul comes home, I always say, 'How was it today? Everything okay?' And if he says, 'Oh, not so good,' right away I'm asking, 'What happened? What's the trouble?' That's because his new boss is rather conservative, and Paul feels he has to push and force issues in order to do his job right. When he tells me things like that, I feel myself tightening up inside and doing everything I can to stay calm. There is this very definite fear that he's going to get fired again, just like his brother was. And yet I don't want him to know I feel that way. I'm sure he does, but I want to hide it."

Even if spouses are not overly worried about future firings, they and their partners frequently need time to put the last one into perspective. For instance, Kevin told us that his wife's dismissal left her with noticeable scars and she is still working hard to reverse the sense of failure and self-doubt brought on by the firing.

Stephanie's husband had been back at work for six months when she told us: "The firing certainly was a positive thing, as far as our relationship goes, but I do feel it has left a definite mark on Alan. Nothing will erase it, not even if he became the president of the corporation. I mean, he's got more than enough to do in his new job, but I think he's still trying to deal with the fact that the people at the other place let him go."

A somewhat similar but more extreme case was reported by Elaine, who has been grappling with the delicate question of just how frail James still is. "He's doing very well now," she says, "but in helping him, I seem to have overdone it. I mean, when he went into the consulting business, I encouraged him to talk about what he was doing every night when he came home. Well, now he's become so self-centered, all he can talk about is himself. He never asks his friends what they are doing, he never asks his kids what they're up to, and he never asks me how I'm feeling. At first, I was afraid if I criticized him in the littlest way I would destroy everything I had accomplished. I'm not so afraid of that any more, and I'm slowly trying to get him to take an interest in other people."

Putting the firing and its long aftermath behind you may also require dealing with whatever anger you may feel toward your partner's former employer. Your anger will not go away simply because your partner gets a new job. Frances, for example, told us that a year after the dismissal she still fantasizes about getting even with the man who fired Nick. And when Clare came to see us, Les had been re-employed for three years, and she was astonished at how bitter she could still feel. "I thought I'd sit down and make a few notes for you, and it all came rushing back," she explained. "The anger's still there and not very far from the surface at all, which really amazed me."

Reflecting on the way he and Irene discharged some of their anger at her former employer, Kevin said, "The settlement they offered her was totally inadequate, given her level and years of service, so we sued. And won. Besides the money, it gave Irene a great feeling that she hadn't just sat back and passively accepted the way they'd shafted her. And I must say I got a rather sweet feeling of revenge, too."

Although Kevin and Irene can take some solace from the fact that they kicked the company where it hurt, we must caution you that lawsuits are not always an effective way of dealing with anger; they are expensive, time-consuming and carry no guarantees. Furthermore, they can easily hobble the job search, which is your partner's first priority.

Interestingly enough, when companies offered fair severance packages, the couples' anger toward the former employers tended to be considerably shorter-lived.

Another bit of emotional debris you may encounter is traces of anger at your partner. Listen to Leslie: "Even in normal times, as a wife and a mother, you feel as though you're constantly giving, and it's the same when he's out of work. You are giving to him, the children, and in a sense you're even giving to your neighbors and your friends, because you're keeping up a facade. I don't know any other way, and that's what I did. But sometimes I was screaming inside and saying, 'Hey, I need, too. Somebody, for crying out loud, talk to me, give to me, too.' "

Spouses automatically take on the task of shepherding their families through the firing and the seemingly interminable job search period. In most cases, they do it willingly and without hesitation, but often at considerable emotional cost. Therefore, when their partners finally do get jobs, they feel a great need for their contributions to be acknowledged.

Leslie simply wanted a "thank-you" from Paul and began to feel that need right after he was re-employed. But with other spouses, this "you owe me" feeling is not an immediate reaction. Rather, at some point in the future, when they need support or extra attention and effort from their partners, they will feel that their partners are now indebted to them and should provide what they need without any question or delay and no hints from them.

The curious thing is that many spouses find it difficult to acknowledge and accept such feelings in themselves. The primary reason is that they gave their support unconditionally and now they feel uncomfortable, perhaps even guilty, about expecting repayment for it. Our response to this dilemma is simple. Your partner is, after all, your partner. Once you have told him or her about your needs it is both fair and understandable to expect reciprocal support.

It is our belief that dealing with such emotional hangovers from the termination is an important part of completing your recovery. For most spouses, simply being aware of these emotions and knowing they are not at all wrong or unusual will be all they need to be able to deal with them. In some cases, though, professional help may be needed to sort out the unresolved issues raised by the termination. The risk lies in not dealing with these issues, which was where we left Linda and her husband, who seem caught in a perpetual Limbo, whether or not he finds a job. "I can only hope things will get better," she says. "We have to get on with our life. Or I have to get on with my life. I don't know what he's going to do."

Hope, however, is usually not enough. Both parties have to want, and to work at, recovery.

Recovering Partners

None of the spouses we talked with could say that absolute bliss and serenity descended upon their households the moment their partners found new jobs. Certainly most of them were extremely pleased, and many were able to tell us how the experience had helped their partners grow and develop.

The happiest results were reported by spouses like Jennifer, whose partners not only found jobs that were a perfect fit, but went into them resolved to maintain a healthy balance between work and family life. In many cases this represented a complete reversal of the partners' previous priorities, which was a clear reflection of the lessons they learned during their periods of unemployment.

Jennifer, for example, is very enthusiastic about Stewart's new job, which is an ideal match of his interests and skills. Moreover, while his old job demanded that he give one hundred and twenty percent all day, every day, his new employers are thrilled to receive one hundred percent, and now he's often home from work before she is. However, she says that the big factor in the change that came over Stewart was the psychological assessment that was part of the outplacement consulting service he received when he was fired. It got right to the heart of the aloofness, impatience and other personal qualities that had caused trouble for him at work and tended to distance him from his family and others.

"It hit the nail right on the head," Jennifer says. "Stewart was amazed at how accurate it was, and he's really been trying to improve. He's not perfect, but he's getting better. For one thing, he isn't so tense, so we're all much more relaxed. And he doesn't just amuse himself with the kids. He's interested in their problems and things like which university our daughter will be going to and what courses she should take, which are things I pretty well used to handle all by myself."

Stewart's type of recovery happened to other job seekers, as well. For example, Kate reported similar growth on the part of Tim, who ended up with a fine job in the financial services industry. It was totally different from the sale of farm machinery, but the vice president who hired him was putting together a team of creative younger people who could bring fresh points of view to the company. Kate believes it was the firing itself that brought out the qualities in Tim that his new employer was looking for. That is, Tim had been hired straight out of business school by the farm machinery manufacturer, which meant that he had never really had to hustle for a job before; and having spent his entire working life in one place, he had never had to display the full range of his skills and interests.

"The firing changed all that," Kate says. "I saw it as soon as he seriously started looking for work. The way he handled the interviews and took calls at home, he was just so much more assertive and aggressive, and he made an astonishing number of good contacts. He's having a ball where he is now, but only the other night, he said, 'I know now that there are a lot of jobs out there.' I mean, he's no longer confined to one company."

Again, it's all a matter of balance and perspective. Vern told us that before Harriet returned to marketing ten years ago, she had a fairly broad-based sense of who she was: a person in her own right, a wife, a mother, a daughter, a friend and so forth. "But once she got wrapped up in her job," Vern said, "her identity was almost totally centered on that. When she was fired, she didn't know who she was any more. She lost all her self-worth, and it took her quite a while to see how narrowly she had defined herself and begin to reevaluate what she had done. Now she has a much deeper understanding of herself and views herself in the context of all her roles and personal qualities, not just what she does at work."

In previous chapters we've seen much the same thing in the way her firing helped Ian's wife, Victoria, get a clearer grasp of what she really values in life. As a result, she has moderated her drive so that her job no longer robs her of valuable time with her husband, family and friends.

Ross had this to say about the effect of Janice's dismissal: "She used to talk about leaving the workforce, or maybe cutting back to three days a week, so she could spend more time with the kids. But now she knows she loves her career and wouldn't be happy working part time. I'd always told her that, but I guess she needed an experience like this to find out for herself. And another thing she's learned is that she only stayed in that other job because she was comfortable, not because she was growing. She's really growing and learning a lot in her new job, but I have a hunch that if she ever feels she's stagnating there, she'll start looking for another, more challenging position right away."

What all these and other former job seekers have in common is that, often to their astonishment, dismissal turned out to be a genuine opportunity to redefine career goals and lifestyle preferences and to find work that was (a) more in keeping with their skills and interests and (b) more consistent with the goals and values they shared with their partners. In short, they are recovering from their firings in the fullest sense of the word, and with their spouses and children are, on the whole, better for it.

Notice that we used the word "recovering." We did not say they have fully recovered, because, after they are re-employed, people are just as vulnerable to continuing doubts and insecurities as their spouses are. For instance, throughout the book, we have been noting how Maggie and her husband, Doug, used the time he was out of work to begin some badly needed repairs on their marriage. Doug is now working at a job they are both very happy about. The work of reshaping their marriage is continuing, and the scope of the task has widened to include Doug's adjustment to his new job and his recovery from the dismissal that began the whole process.

Like Maggie and Doug, Kevin and Irene now spend a lot of time discussing the politics of the new job. Their relationship is a lot easier now that Irene is no longer working in Kevin's home-based insurance brokerage, which is a mixed blessing. "The fact is," Kevin told us, "we're not seeing a whole lot of each other. Irene's working long hours, learning her new job, putting her team together and generally trying to establish her credibility, and when she is at home, she's busy seeing the household is in order and trying to spend as much time with the kids as possible. The trouble is, right now, she doesn't have that much time, so she's always tired, and I know she feels guilty about not being with me and the kids as much as we'd like."

This is a common phenomenon. In addition to their jobs, most women also carry the major responsibility for organizing their homes and ensuring that their children's needs are met. Although the husbands we interviewed helped a lot, they acknowledged that the question of finding a good balance between work and home was a major problem for their wives. This was especially true when they were adjusting to the demands of a new job. While happy to be reemployed, they were also prey to stress and guilt at not being able to give as much of themselves as they wanted to their families. As Kevin put it, "It's important for me to remember that Irene is really carrying two full time jobs. It's easy for me to forget that, but she needs me to support her, understand the stress she's under and anticipate and do things that will take some of the pressure off."

Recovering Finances

We encountered some couples who were able to use the severance money to pay off their mortgages and other debts. There were many men and women who ended up in better-paying jobs.

Of course there were also some who took jobs that paid salaries lower than what they had previously been earning. Here one of two things happened. If the new job was a good fit and the person happy in it, the reduced salary was not a big issue. As one woman said, "It just means you have to wait longer to buy things." On the other hand, if the job was a bad fit and the person unhappy in it, the resulting squeeze on his or her family's spending habits became a burden, because the sacrifices seemed to be pointless.

We also interviewed a few couples who were faced with the repayment of debts they had incurred during the job search. Others were still upset that they had been forced to dip into their savings. If the job search turned out well, many couples regarded their borrowing or spent savings as good investments, but almost all resented being forced to take those measures at all.

This is one of the big reasons why, during the recovery period, many couples begin to develop new financial strategies and establish contingency funds to meet unexpected events. It both augments their sense of personal security and allows them to feel more in charge of their lives and careers.

Earlier in this book we mentioned that Nick was forced out of the insurance firm where he had worked for twenty-five years. He ended up with a somewhat better job and an increased salary, but he and his wife, Frances, are now aware that people can no longer be guaranteed perpetual employment. "To us, this new job's very much a temporary thing," Frances says. "We're not cruising along like we were before, saying, 'Okay, we're all set till he's sixty-five.' We've taken a close look at our finances and opened a special account to put money aside for emergencies. Nick says he'd like to stay with the firm for at least two years, though he might be there for five. By then, he'll have made lots of contacts and he can go into consulting if he wants, or maybe he'll want to take early retirement. We're preparing for both options and whatever other surprises life has in store for us."

Recovering Families

As we have been seeing throughout this book, having either parent around more than usual forced entire families to communicate in ways that were hitherto impossible. To be sure, this sometimes resulted in much stress, as in the case of Karen and Gil or Linda and Ben and their families, for example. But, overall, we believe that the experience can lead to stronger ties between parents and children and husbands and wives. In fact, some spouses find themselves wondering whether their partners' return to work will bring an end to these changes.

In Ross's case it did, and he was very upset by the long hours Janice had to spend on her new job. "I knew she was trying to prove herself and that there were major changes occurring in the company she had overall responsibility for," Ross said. "But she was spending four nights a week there. I began to worry that she was becoming totally career-oriented and forgetting about her family. She kept telling me things would get better, but I didn't see it happening. Then one night we had a big blow-up. She said she needed me to understand and support her and, if I couldn't, I could at least get off her back. That's when I realized the huge stress she was under. So I backed off and started looking for ways I could help her, and I think I've done pretty well at that. Anyway, now she's the one who's complaining about the hours and I'm the one who's always saying things will get better."

For her part, although Jennifer is confident that the new relationship with Stewart will continue, she is ready to act if there is any sign that it might be in jeopardy. "The only thing

I think could happen," she says, "is that he'll get so involved in his new job he'll go back to being as tense as he was before. If he does, I think I'll be more inclined to say, 'Hey, do you realize that this is starting to happen again, and we've all agreed that it has all worked out for the best and we like it the way it is?' "

Despite the frequent storms and pain that went with her husband's period of unemployment and the many anxieties that still plague her, Leslie is yet another spouse who believes the crisis had a positive side. "Paul and I have learned to be very open with each other," she says. "We've learned to be open with the children, and we found out the true meaning of friends. What happens is that all of a sudden you realize life isn't just money. I didn't think that before Paul was fired, but a sudden lack of money makes you realize that you have to sit down and really dig deep and think about your priorities. I mean, you really have to sit down and look at yourself as a person and as a member of a family."

For Vern and Harriet, her job loss brought about a subtle but welcome change in their relationship. "When I lost my job ten years ago," Vern explained, "I think Harriet was disappointed in the change it brought to our lifestyle. I think she no longer saw me as the white knight who could provide everything she wanted. But since she lost her job, she's started to see me in terms of what I do provide, rather than what I don't. She seems to accept me more for who I am and appreciates the support and encouragement I've given her so she can do the things she wants. In a quiet, accepting way, our relationship is stronger and warmer than ever."

And then there is Cheryl, who went into the paper-recycling business with her husband. At the start, she still deeply regretted losing the wealth and perks that had gone with Glen's previous position, and she was extremely leery about the risks inherent in the new venture. When we talked to her three years later, though, her attitude about family and money had undergone a remarkable change.

"We made a bit of money in the first year," she says, "so that was a help. But the main thing was, I could see a great difference in Glen's happiness. After another year or so, I turned around and all of a sudden I thought, this is great. Working together is really fun. I'm enjoying what I'm doing. We'd been so busy, I hadn't really had time to think about it. By then, the kids were helping out on weekends and getting quite involved in the company, so it was a real family effort. And it was at that point that I suddenly thought, life is going on, so why am I still festering about what happened in the past? Why not leave it behind? And I've pretty well managed to do that."

Recovering Spouses

In previous chapters, we talked about how some spouses responded to their partners' terminations by becoming more cautious about their own jobs and career objectives. One of these was Cynthia. Her husband is now in consulting, which she cannot yet bring herself to believe is a secure profession. As a result, she now regards herself as the family's major breadwinner and feels she has to stay in her job, ignoring any potential career moves that may come her way. The fact that she and Lloyd are actually in very good financial shape and that she speaks of her attitude as being "trapped in my head" raises the hope that she will become more adventurous as she gets used to Lloyd's new situation.

With Irene back at work, Kevin once again has his home-based insurance brokerage to himself. He is delighted, but he has also learned an important lesson: "Many of the things Irene wanted me to change were warranted," he says. "We fought over some of them, and I implemented them rather grudgingly, but they're working fabulously. She is a great organizer, and I discovered I can learn from her. To do that, all I had to do was listen to her advice without letting my ego get in the way and automatically interpreting everything she said as personal criticism."

In contrast to Cynthia, Jennifer has actually been liberated by her husband's new attitude toward work and now feels profoundly more independent in her own profession, which she practices on a free-lance basis. "Right now, there's a crisis at the place where I'm working," she says, "and I'm thinking if things don't go my way, I can just leave and go somewhere else. A year ago, I wouldn't have dared to think that."

Cheryl has achieved a similar perspective. "Money's just not as important to me as it once was," she says. "It's nice. But I have the confidence now that we can go out and earn what we need to make our life comfortable, live the life that we want to live, and it isn't with a big corporation. So we've come a long way."

Using Cheryl and Jennifer as only two of several possible examples, we can say that an ideal recovery is essentially a process by which spouses, both as individuals and as marital partners, take advantage of the opportunity provided by their mates' firing to reassess their goals and values. They may, for example, decide that they have been on the path that is best for them all along and emerge from the termination crisis with a strengthened understanding of their own needs and an increased commitment to their ways of doing things and approaching life. Then again, they may conclude that changes are needed and begin to make them.

Recovering Children

The new routines that come with a parent's return to work can be especially difficult for children who have enjoyed having Mom or Dad at home. For example, after Irene started work, her daughter refused to speak to her for two days. However, with a little time and a lot of sensitivity on the parents' part, kids generally adapt quite well.

We advise that you help your kids anticipate and prepare for the changes that will occur when Mom or Dad returns to work. Above all, it's important to maintain improvements made in parent-child relationships during the job search period. This is often a very simple thing to do. For instance, one newly hired man made a point of spending time alone with each of his children every day. As he explained it, "I've come to realize that the company doesn't count the extra hours I spend at work, but my kids sure do."

Lessons Learned

As we said at the beginning of this chapter, family members who were just embarking on the recovery process frequently spoke of needing time to put the firing and its aftermath into perspective. Those who had already had time to do that were able to articulate a number of lessons they had learned from the termination experience.

Now We Know Who Our Friends Are

This space is devoted to Maggie and Doug, who learned the hard way about false friendships. "I'm not saying I'm cynical about people now," Maggie explains. "But I'm probably more sensitive to what they say and just how good a friend they are. Years ago, Doug told me some of the people he worked with were only superficial friends, and I said, 'Oh, no, they're not. They're all right at heart.' But it turned out they weren't. I don't mean I'm not trusting my friends. I do, but I'm listening more carefully to what they say."

It's Great to be Out of the Squirrel Cage

A very large number of spouses reported that after the shock of the firing and the job search period were over, they began to realize that they and their partners were better off, now that they no longer had to endure the tensions and turmoil that characterized life in their partners' previous workplaces. Here's how Cheryl described it: "It's so far in the past now, I really don't think about the company any more, though you do hear things. There's been another new president, and the company itself has been sold, so the insanity there is just as great as ever, and I found myself feeling sorry for all the unhappy people who are still working in that building."

No One is Indispensable

Stephanie stated this lesson very simply: "Life goes on without you. That accounting firm certainly didn't fall apart when they laid Alan off." Mary Beth was more reflective, partly because she's a high-level manager herself and partly because her husband would, in all probability, have been president of his company had it not been sold. "No matter what level you're at," she now says, "you're just a number, and regardless of how hard you work, if circumstances change, or if there's a change of management, or your corporation is being taken over, you could be on your way out the door. Even if someone just doesn't like your personality, you might not be fired, but you could be demoted. So it's foolish to think your job is the be-all and end-all. Even Martin's friends are now saying, 'What happened to you could happen to me.' "

She couldn't be more right. One of the central lessons taught by today's job market is that the only security is within yourself, not in any company. At its most basic, this means that your skills and knowledge must always be up to date. If they are, and you find that one company no longer needs what you have to offer, there will be others that do.

Watch for Signs That All Is Not Well

One surprising tendency we noticed was that despite the vivid reminders they received when they were fired, as soon as they are settled into a new job, some people appear to forget that neither they nor anyone else in a corporation is indispensable. They revert to behavior that may have contributed to their firing and, once again, ignore signals that trouble could be brewing. Their spouses, on the other hand, usually don't forget, and many become very watchful, closely monitoring the politics of their partners' new workplaces, ever on the alert for signs that things are not going well.

At the beginning of this chapter we cited Leslie's fears about the consequences of Paul's conflicts with his new boss. Her concern was completely justified. Paul was fired a few months later. However, he very quickly got another job, which was a much better fit, so the anxiety that followed his second firing was not as prolonged as it was after the first one.

The Right Job Is Better Than Just Any Job

Stephanie is picking up similar signals to the ones Leslie received. However, apart from her concern for Alan, she is not overly worried, because she has been able not only to read the writing on the wall, but also combine the message with a far more important lesson she learned in the aftermath of her husband's firing. That is, if your partner's new job is a poor fit and he or she is miserable in it, there are no long-term benefits in having him or her stay there.

As she explains it: "In this new job, he seems to be getting involved in a lot of personality clashes of one kind or another. But I think the root of it all is that those people have a totally different way of looking at and doing things, and it's hard for him to adapt to that. If he finds it's getting too heavy, I'll have no hesitation about saying, 'Okay, look elsewhere.' I probably wouldn't have said that before he was let go from his previous job, but now I firmly believe it. Earlier I might have just said, 'Hang in there. It's a job. Keep on bringing that paycheck home.' Now I've learned."

Above All, Don't Ignore Yourself

During a termination crisis, your partner will likely require an enormous amount of support, and although you will freely provide it, it's crucial to keep a balance between the support you give him or her and the support you give to yourself. Spouses, as well as job seekers, need to have their own action plans for surviving the crisis, and spouses who don't have such plans and devote all their energy to helping their partners, risk becoming too caught up in the partners' emotions at the expense of their own identities.

Mary Ellen instinctively avoided that trap. After her husband was fired, he wanted her to cut down her volunteer work and look after him. She didn't, and the result has been twofold. One, she is a stronger, richer person in her own right; and two, her strength and resources have had an increasingly beneficial effect on his way of looking at life. As far as his job search goes, he is now genuinely in transition and is taking a close, unhurried look at three possible career options. "And when you get right down to it," Mary Ellen says, "it is the children and I who are giving him his opportunity. We are giving him this chance to go out and look at his options in complete freedom."

In vivid contrast to Mary Ellen is Elaine. To be sure, she helped pull James out of his depression and encouraged him in the start of his new business, and she is very proud of what she has done. But, as we noted earlier in this chapter, he never asks how she is feeling. As she bluntly told us, "I think I tried so hard to encourage him that I went a little bit overboard, by not balancing it with having an interesting life of my own." Determined to do something about it, Elaine now works part time as an interior decorator and serves on the acquisitions committee of her local art gallery. She and her husband are also thinking about their priorities as a couple.

Elaine has no doubts about the future or regrets about the past. "You know," she said, "we do have a wonderful marriage, because I truly do love him, and he absolutely adores me, and that's a wonderful thing to be able to say after thirty-two years. He often tells me, 'I don't know where I'd be if it weren't for you,' and that makes me feel strong. I've had people say to me, 'I don't know how you've stuck with him all these years.' To me, that's an utterly ridiculous thing to say. I mean, what do you promise when you get married? Through better, through worse, through richer, through poorer. It's not all a bowl of cherries. Nobody said it was."

We must provide you with one more warning: Take good care of yourself *after* your partner finds a job. Some spouses told us that the stress of the termination crisis did not really take hold of them until the job search was over. As one woman said, "I was able to make it through the search period and find the resources I needed to cope with my own uncertainties and support my husband. But after he was back at work for four months, I became quite ill and somewhat depressed. My doctor said it was a delayed reaction. Once Roger was working again, I guess my defences relaxed and all the tension caught up with me."

We Can Do it!

Earlier we explained that the foundation of Stephanie's new attitude is her and her husband's confidence that having coped with and survived one termination crisis, they can do it again if necessary. Looking back over the whole experience, Sheila exclaimed, "It was a positive thing. These things can happen, and I'm aware of that now. Before it never entered my mind. But now I know it can happen to us. If it happens again, we'll know we've lived through it once, so we can live through it again."

Thus, paradoxically, while the firing may have given couples their first intimation of just how vulnerable they are in today's business climate, it also revealed their resilience and joint strengths. As Leslie said, "We dug deep and we made it."

I Can Do It!

During a termination crisis, a great number of spouses discover that they do have the inner strength, skills and confidence to survive and grow in their own right. We have, for example, seen how Pat found the strength and the time to return to school to learn new skills. We have seen how Elaine had to struggle to pull her husband through his illness and coax him into a brand-new business. She is now very proud, not only of what she did, but also of the way she proved to herself and to her critical family that she could more than survive.

Similarly, Agnes took a job just before Earl's dismissal and stuck with it, even though she suffered a lengthy illness. The whole experience has been unremittingly tough on her, but she is very proud of the way she has managed.

When Victoria was first looking for work, Ian paid more attention to the details of her job search than the empathy and understanding she needed. His reason for doing so was that he was afraid his sympathy would merely encourage her to wallow in her emotions, when her first task was to find a job. Therefore, he pressed her to be more aggressive in her search and was impatient when she wanted to air her emotions. Only gradually did he see that expressing her feelings was Victoria's way of healing the wounds caused by her dismissal. "I finally got it," Ian said. "All she really needed was for me to listen and reassure her that she was okay and everything would work out. Whenever I did that, she began to feel better and after an hour or so, she'd get back to looking for a job." He is rightly proud of how he learned to help Victoria deal with the emotional side effects of her job loss and the enormous contribution he made to her ultimate success.

For her part, Stephanie took a part-time job after her husband was fired, primarily to keep herself busy and out of the house and, of course, to help out with the family finances. She now has a full-time job, and the income and security it provides is what makes her willingness to see Alan through another job search, a practical proposition.

Then there is Cheryl, who is both pleased with and a trifle astonished at the skills and confidence she developed over the three years it took her and Glen to build up their business. "That first year," she says, "we worked so many long hours, I don't know how we did it. But we did it together. We're partners all the way down the line. People I've met through the business have offered me a couple of really neat jobs. I've turned them down. It's exciting to know I've been retrained and people think I'm employable, but I want my own business now."

We met many spouses who, confronted with their partners' dismissals, reached for the best in themselves and found it. While very often juggling the needs of their jobs, households, children and partners, they found the inner strength and resources to contend with their circumstances, struggle with their own emotions and emerge from it all somehow stronger.

At the beginning of the book we noted that spouses are too often the unacknowledged and unappreciated "invisible partners" in their mates' careers. However, it is extremely difficult for someone who has been through a termination crisis to continue to ignore his or her spouse's contributions to their partnership.

We hope the day is not far off when the spouse's family, friends, colleagues and the business community as a whole recognize those contributions, as well. For now though, we hope you will accept this book as our personal recognition of, and tribute to, your efforts, your strengths and your successes.

Further Reading

Bolles, Richard Nelson. *The 1993 What Color Is Your Parachute? A Practical Manual for Job-Hunters and Career Changers.* Berkeley, California: Ten Speed Press, 1993.

_____. *The New Quick Job-Hunting Map: How to Create a Picture of Your Ideal Job or Next Career.* Berkeley, California: Ten Speed Press, 1990.

Davis, Paul D. *When Your Corporate Umbrella Begins to Leak.* Bethesda, Maryland: National Press Books, 1991.

DeRoche, Frederick W., and Mary A. McDougall. *Now It's Your Move: A Guide for the Outplaced Employee.* Englewood Cliffs, New Jersey: Prentice-Hall, 1984.

Gottlieb, Linda, and Carole Hyatt. *When Smart People Fail.* New York: Simon and Schuster, 1987; Penguin Books, 1988.

Hunt, Bernice, and Clifford J. Sager. *Intimate Partners: Hidden Patterns in Love Relationships.* New York: McGraw-Hill, 1979.

Kushner, Harold. S. *When Bad Things Happen to Good People.* New York: Avon Books, 1981.

Lerner, Harriet Goldhor. *The Dance of Anger: A Woman's Guide to Changing the Patterns of Intimate Relationships.* New York: Harper and Row, 1985.

_____. *The Dance of Intimacy: A Woman's Guide to Courageous Acts of Change in Key Relationships.* New York: Harper and Row, 1989.

Payne, Richard. *How to Get a Better Job Quicker*. New York: Mentor Books, 1987.

Robinson, Jo, and Jean Staeheli. *Unplug the Christmas Machine*. New York: Quill, an imprint of William Morrow, 1982.

The following set of pamphlets by Nancy Ervin can be purchased for $5 U.S or $6 Canadian from Conquest Corporation, P.O. Box 1090, Birminham, Michigan 48102; telehone (313) 646-1344.

The package includes:

- *Kids on the Move: A Parental Guide to Help Your Child Relocate*
- *Teen Talk: Straight Talk about Moving; One Teen to Another*
- *Tips for Every Relocating Spouse*

About the Authors

Jill Jukes is a Senior Consultant with Murray Axmith & Associates Ltd., one of North America's premier career transition consulting firms. She has had extensive experience in corporate human resources management, particularly manpower planning, training and development, and counseling.

Ruthan Rosenberg is the Director of Program Development at Murray Axmith & Associates Ltd., where she is responsible for developing new services and resources for job seekers. She has designed and implemented employee assistance counseling programs and has worked as a professional counselor in both the private and the public sector.